The **ESOP**
Committee
Guide

THIRD EDITION

Randy,
The Retirement Plan Committee is excited that you agreed to volunteer for the inagural Communication Committee. Your leadership will help to establish the foundation for what we all expect to be a highly successful company for years to come.
Thanks for all that you do for RiverWood Bank.
Paul Meum

The **ESOP**
Committee
Guide

THIRD EDITION

Jim Bado
Stephen Clifford
Dave Fitz-Gerald
Brian A. Inniger
Camille Kerr
Kellee Kroll
Linshuang Lu
Christopher Mackin
Liz McKeever
Alexander Moss
Tracey Myers
The Phelps County Bank ESOP Committee
Loren Rodgers
Corey Rosen
Virginia Vanderslice
Jack Veale

The National Center for Employee Ownership
Oakland, California

This publication is designed to provide accurate and authoritative information in regard to the subject matter covered. It is sold with the understanding that the publisher is not engaged in rendering legal, accounting, or other professional service. If legal advice or other expert assistance is required, the services of a competent professional person should be sought.

Legal, accounting, and other rules affecting business often change. Before making decisions based on the information you find here or in any publication from any publisher, you should ascertain what changes might have occurred and what changes might be forthcoming. The NCEO's Web site (including the members-only area) and newsletter for members provide regular updates on these changes. If you have any questions or concerns about a particular issue, check with your professional advisor or, if you are an NCEO member, call or email us.

The ESOP Committee Guide, 3rd ed.

Book design by Scott Rodrick.

The National Center for Employee Ownership
1629 Telegraph Ave., Suite 200
Oakland, CA 94612
(510) 208-1300
(510) 272-9510 (fax)
Web site: www.nceo.org

ISBN-10: 1-932924-85-X
ISBN-13: 978-1-932924-85-5

Contents

Preface

Loren Rodgers

Writing about ESOP committees is like writing about art. Art is a vast, diverse field, and everyone has individual ideas about what makes good art. Many people have strong opinions and intricately reasoned arguments supporting those opinions. The same challenges face someone trying to make sense of the best way to establish, maintain, or restart an ESOP committee. On the other hand, with art as well as ESOP committees, some ideas stand the test of time.

This book is the NCEO's attempt to present the best thinking there is on ESOP committees. We intend this book to be a resource for members of committees or for people who interact with committees. It is appropriate for people just getting started in the ESOP world and for professionals seeking to ensure they have covered all their bases.

Maybe your company is thinking of establishing a committee, or maybe you already have one but think it could use a helping hand to become more effective. Maybe your committee has seen better days, or maybe you see nothing but blue skies ahead. No matter what situation you are in, this book will give you tested ideas from successful ESOP committees and insights from seasoned advisors that will expand your thinking about the possibilities for your company's ESOP committee.

Some ESOP committees are administrative committees that focus on plan operations or the management of plan assets. These committees are either "administrative committees" or "fiduciary committees," and this book discusses them in chapters 1, 2, and 9. Most of this book covers "communications committees," groups that focus on building communication, education and culture.

Part 1 of this book, "The Roles of ESOP Committees," begins with an overview chapter providing a survey of the types of ESOP committees, the core principles that make them succeed, and the basic structural issues in setting committees up for success. Chapter 2 covers the basic duties of an ESOP administrative committee, while chapter 3 discusses some of the creative activities that communications committees may do.

Part 2, "Best Practices," begins with chapter 4, on developing key committee parameters. Chapter 5 presents a thought-provoking approach to leadership, aimed both at helping company leaders work effectively with ESOP committees and at giving committee leaders the tools they need. Chapter 6 takes a life-cycle view of ESOP committees, while chapter 7 covers nine typical problems of ESOP committees.

Part 3 presents case studies. Chapter 8 begins with an in-depth case study of the BL Companies ESOP committee, followed by an analysis of the completely different paths taken at two other successful companies, Gardener's Supply and Fortsythe Technology. Finally, chapter 9 covers five companies and their ESOP committees. The case studies are intentionally diverse and include both communication committees and an administrative committee. These case studies will broaden your perspective for the possible scope of an ESOP committee.

Part 1

The Roles of ESOP Committees

CHAPTER 1

ESOP Committees: An Overview

Alexander P. Moss, Virginia J. Vanderslice, and Linshuang Lu

ESOP committees fulfill different roles at different companies. Some are legal committees that advise and/or direct the ESOP trustees on fiduciary issues relating directly to the ESOP. Other committees provide opportunities for employees to train, educate, and communicate ownership messages to employees, and/or to advise senior leadership on operational and business issues. An ESOP committee's goals should inform its structure and membership composition.

This chapter provides an overview of ESOP committees: their goals, the scope of their activities, their membership composition, their evaluation, and the resources required for them to function optimally.

What Is an ESOP Committee?

An ESOP committee can be any group of employees assigned to any set of legally permissible ESOP and ownership-related tasks in an ESOP company. ESOP committees differ from other types of employee committees in that they support the achievement of a company's ownership objectives. This definition includes a wide variety of committees with different responsibilities.

Companies have different ownership objectives that support their overall strategic direction in varying ways. Ownership objectives may be financial, but they may also be cultural and operational. Some examples include:

- increase the value of the ESOP for employees and retirees
- encourage "ownership thinking" for all employees, allowing them to take initiative to solve customer and company problems
- foster "ownership behaviors" for all employees by improving everyday behaviors that support business goals

Because ESOP committees support the company's ownership objectives, which differ from company to company, ESOP committees can vary widely in activities and structure. Nevertheless, ESOP committees typically have one or more of the following objectives:

- to provide *fiduciary direction* to the ESOP trustee
- to serve as *ESOP advocates*, communicating the ESOP and keeping employee ownership visible to the workforce as a whole
- to make *recommendations to senior leadership* about various ESOP-related issues
- to provide *two-way communications* between employee-owners and senior leadership
- to contribute directly to *improving business performance* and achieving the company's strategic goals

Depending on the goals, ESOP committees may be engaged in various activities:

- *education:* ESOP education and training for employees, financial literacy education
- *motivation/celebration:* celebrations, awards, event planning
- *communication:* gathering employee input, providing feedback to senior leadership
- *advisory:* making recommendations to senior leadership about employee-related issues

This list of goals is not exhaustive—other objectives are certainly permissible, within existing legal constraints (mostly legal restraints arising from pension and labor law). Although these goals share similar elements, they may result in distinct activities and responsibilities for the ESOP committee. Committee goals may be captured in a formal mission statement and/or charter, or maintained informally in committee records. ESOP committees may also be called different names, such as "Ownership Committee," "ESOP Communications Committee," "ESOP Advisory Council," "Employee Ownership Team," or "ESOP Fiduciary Committee." These names often indicate the committee's objectives and responsibilities. Whatever the case, committee members should understand the committee's objectives and be clear about what they are trying to accomplish.

The Big Picture: Linking Ownership to Improved Performance

ESOP committees often play a key role in creating an ownership culture to drive business performance. Many companies try to cultivate an ownership culture, where employees think and act like owners—they take responsibility for their own jobs, understand the business, take initiatives to improve the company performance, and provide input into decisions that affect them.

Research completed during the last 20 years consistently indicates that employee ownership is clearly associated with business performance improvement. However, sharing stock ownership alone does not improve company performance as measured by sales growth, growth in the number of employees, or operating cash flow performance. Researchers have found a more specific link: those companies that *combine employee ownership with participation* perform better than they did before implementing an ESOP, and they perform better than similar companies that are not employee-owned.[1]

These results indicate that ESOP companies that implement key elements of creating an ownership culture (e.g., sharing company strategies and financial information, employee business training, opportunities for employees to have input into daily job decisions, or team-based decision-making) experience performance improve-

---

1. See the studies summarized in *Employee Ownership and Corporate Performance*, 2011 revision (Oakland, CA: NCEO, 2011).

ments greater than those of comparison companies. The data make it clear that employee ownership can provide substantial financial gains for companies beyond tax benefits. These performance improvements, however, are not automatic—they can be achieved only with employee engagement and participation.

An ESOP committee can contribute to improving company performance as part of an overall effort to build an "ownership culture." Many companies have achieved significant success in this effort—several are profiled later in this book. ESOP committees have been explicitly designed, supported, evaluated, and modified over time to focus on performance improvement goals that support each company's overall strategic ownership objectives. Some provide education and training around understanding financial information so that employees know how their behavior affects company performance, while others provide employees an opportunity to give input into operational strategy.

The development of an ownership culture is a complex and lengthy process, and a full discussion of these challenges is beyond the scope of this chapter.[2] This chapter will mention the opportunities and challenges in using your ESOP committee as part of a broader strategy to create an ownership culture. The ESOP committee by itself, even at its most effective, is only one component in the broader process.

How Do the Core Principles for All Teams Apply to ESOP Committees?

Because an ESOP committee is a group of individuals working together, the basic principles of effective teams apply to ESOP committees. To function effectively, ESOP committees should have the following characteristics:

---

2.   For more information on how to develop an ownership culture, see "Building Long-Term Value: Developing a High-Performance Ownership Culture" by Virginia J. Vanderslice and Alexander P. Moss, available at http://www.praxiscg. com/published-work/building-long-term-value-developing-high-performance-ownership-culture.

- *Goals.* ESOP committees should be established to meet specific goals. All of the other committee characteristics, such as its membership, authority and responsibilities, depend on these core objectives.

- *Structure.* ESOP committees should be structured appropriately to meet their goals—the number of members, member qualifications and representation (both individually and for the committee as a whole), member selection, subcommittees, decision-making, and other operational processes should support effective achievement of committee goals.

- *Resources.* ESOP committees should have access to the resources necessary to achieve their goals. In addition to the time commitment to conduct committee work and appropriate funding, members should have access to relevant information and access to individuals representing other functions within the company, such as senior leadership, finance, human resources, and operations.

- *Evaluation.* ESOP committees should be evaluated and modified as their environment and/or goals evolve over time. This evaluation should be conducted by the committee itself and by its organizational sponsor—whomever the ESOP committee reports to.

The remainder of this chapter addresses how these general issues are applied in the context of different ESOP committees.

Types of ESOP Committees

There are three common types of ESOP committees that may be distinguished by the nature of their duties and the source of their authority: ESOP administrative/fiduciary committees, ESOP communications committees, and labor-management ESOP committees with negotiated authority.

Type 1: ESOP Fiduciary and Administrative Committees

ESOP fiduciary and administrative committees focus on decision-making and administration relating to the ESOP plan itself. ESOP fiduciary committees advise the ESOP trustee in making decisions about the ESOP itself, from purchasing and selling shares to select-ing professional advisors, rather than advising company leadership about ownership communications and/or company operations. In general, fiduciary committees have specific legal obligations and constraints and are "named fiduciaries" under the Employee Re-tirement Income Security Act (ERISA).[3] Fiduciary committees are most common when the ESOP trustee is an external party (often a trust company affiliated with a bank), rather than an inside party. Figure 1-1 illustrates the position of an ESOP fiduciary committee in the company's overall governance structure.

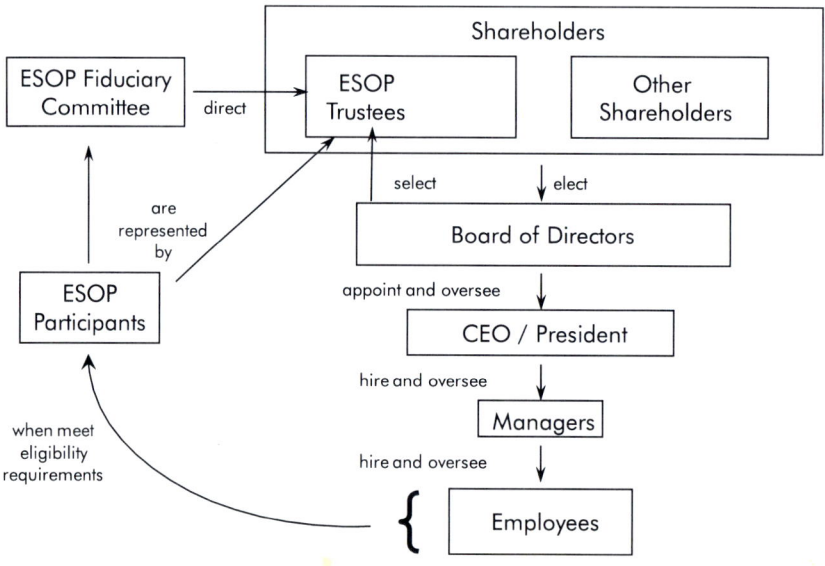

Figure 1-1. Sample company structure with ESOP fiduciary committee

An ESOP administrative committee focuses on the operation of the plan and on the management of plan assets. This type of committee may or may not be a named fiduciary in the ESOP plan, depending on its range of responsibilities and authority, and it may have only advisory power and no formal authority to make decisions

---

3.   A complete description of these ERISA duties is well beyond the scope of this chapter, but additional information is available in chapter 2 of this book and in Dina Schlossberg and James Steiker, "ESOP Fiduciary Committees," *Journal of Employee Ownership Law and Finance* 12, no. 3 (summer 2000).

regarding the ESOP. While some administrative committees are not named fiduciaries, they may still intentionally or unintentionally act as fiduciaries depending on the types of decisions they make and actions they take. All committees involved with any aspect of managing or decision-making regarding ESOP plan assets should regularly consult legal counsel to understand their range of duties and to avoid unintentional legal liability.

ERISA requires that ESOPs must have trustees, but ESOP companies are not required to have ESOP fiduciary or administrative committees. Many ESOP plan documents refer to an "ESOP Committee." In most cases this refers to the committee with specific ESOP fiduciary and/or administrative functions, not the broader communications functions. Many ESOP companies do not want their less formal ESOP committees to make fiduciary decisions or manage plan assets. The essential point is that an ESOP fiduciary and administrative committee often serves in a formal legal capacity, and the responsibilities (and risks) borne by the committee are regulated under ERISA.

It is critical not to confuse this type of ESOP committee with the other types, which advise *company leadership* (rather than advising the ESOP trustees) on various *company issues* (rather than ESOP trust issues) and which generally are not fiduciaries and do not face the same level of regulatory scrutiny and risk. Issues facing ESOP fiduciaries, including fiduciary committees, are addressed in many other venues in the ESOP community. While these issues are not the main focus of the remainder of this chapter, we will identify some of the distinctions as we discuss issues addressed by other kinds of ESOP committees.

Type 2: ESOP Communications Committee

In contrast to an ESOP fiduciary and/or administrative committee, an ESOP communications committee is often an advisory body to management on various ESOP-related communications issues. The committee may have explicit authority to develop its own budget and conduct a broad range of tasks, such as delivering ownership and/or business training, conducting new employee orientations, publishing newsletters, soliciting employee input on various operating and/or employee policy issues, and/or other communications tasks.

ESOP communications committees are accountable to senior leadership. With a few exceptions, discussed below, company leadership can delegate any of its powers and duties to the ESOP communications committee. This differs profoundly from an ESOP fiduciary committee, which gets its authority from the ESOP document and whose powers and duties are regulated by ERISA (characterized as a "Type 1" committee above). Figure 1-2 illustrates the position of an ESOP communications committee in the company's overall governance structure.

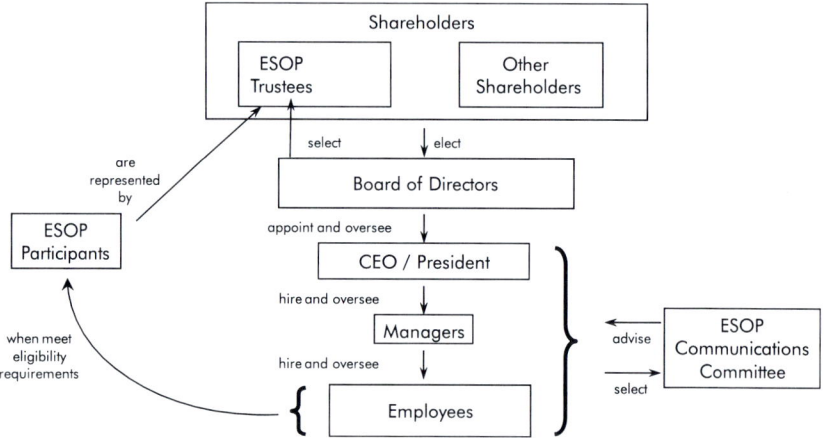

Figure 1-2. Sample company structure with ESOP communications committee

It may be obvious, but always worth repeating, that management cannot delegate any of its powers and duties to the ESOP communications committee that would violate the law or regulatory limitations. For instance, management may not delegate to the ESOP communications committee any powers that would, in effect, establish a union under the National Labor Relations Act (NLRA, the federal law that governs labor-management relations). For example, if management appoints a committee that includes both managers and nonmanagers and delegates to this committee the formal authority for making decisions about wages, hours, and/ or other terms and conditions of employment, this may be interpreted as creating a "company union," and should be avoided, as these types of negotiations may generally be conducted only in the context of collective bargaining. The broader point is that ESOP companies should be aware that there are some limits on what they can do and should seek appropriate legal advice to avoid inadvertent regulatory conflicts.

Some ESOP communications committee may have no formal authority at all, and may serve solely as an advisory committee to senior management (or to management and labor leadership). Some companies are most comfortable with this structure because it does not create as much confusion over decision-making. An ESOP communications committee with no formal power can generally make recommendations on a variety of issues. Because it does not make final decisions, it can be flexible and can become involved in many policy areas. It may make recommendations including the types of ownership and business training needed, how best to design and deliver such training, changes to the ESOP plan to address employee concerns (such as concerns regarding eligibility and vesting requirements), operational issues concerning improving business performance, and even governance issues including various board of directors decisions and/or ESOP trustee decisions. This committee does not offer binding advice but rather serves as a two-way communications channel between employees and leadership and governance bodies. (See figure 1-2.)

Whenever this type of committee reaches an internal decision, it simply sends its recommendation to leadership for review and approval. Other companies find that this limits the effectiveness of the ESOP committee and places additional burdens on leaders to review recommendations and actions that might be more efficiently delegated to the committee within reasonable limits. As a result, many companies prefer to delegate limited but meaningful authority to their committees. An ESOP committee may have authority in some areas (e.g. relating to ESOP education) and only an advisory role in other areas (e.g. benefits, and/or operational performance enhancement opportunities).

Type 3: Joint Labor-Management ESOP Committee, with Negotiated Authority

Companies whose employees are represented by unions under collective bargaining agreements often negotiate the powers of the ESOP committee and related issues.[4] The resulting ESOP committee tends to reflect the broader relationship between labor and management in an ESOP company.

When the union has had little or no role in the ESOP and it prefers to bargain for non-ESOP benefits. In these cases, the ESOP committee looks very similar to the other types described above with little, if any, union involvement. The primary difference is that management may not delegate to the ESOP committee any powers or duties that may have been reserved for labor and management under the collective bargaining agreement. In other words, the ESOP and the collective bargaining agreement cover different issues, and the ESOP committee may not infringe on collective bargaining issues.

When the union is actively involved in establishing or operating the ESOP. Participation by bargaining unit members in the ESOP is much more common, and the terms of their participation in the ESOP may be bargained within the framework of the NLRA. This process does not require an ESOP committee, but labor and management may negotiate whether to have an ESOP fiduciary committee, an administrative committee, and/or an ESOP communications committee, as well as their respective roles and members. In these cases, the ESOP committee, whatever its form, assumes authority delegated to it by the collective bargaining process (rather than by management alone). It is therefore accountable to both labor and management under the terms of their agreement.

---

4.   A full discussion of labor-management issues in ESOP companies is beyond the scope of this overview. Further information is available through the Ohio Employee Ownership Center at Kent State University.

ESOP Committees Should Be Structured Appropriately to Meet Their Goals

Once the purposes for the ESOP committee are clear, its structure should be designed accordingly. The committee's structure includes aspects such as the number of members, the criteria for membership—both for individual members and for the overall composition of the committee, the selection process for members, and the committee's decision-making processes. Chapters 4 and 5 of this book have more information on structuring committees, but because fiduciary/administrative and communication committees have significant different objectives, they will be discussed separately in this chapter. Because joint labor-management committees tend to take the form of either a fiduciary/administrative committee or an ESOP communications committee, they will be mentioned in the context of the other two types of committees.

ESOP Fiduciary and Administrative Committees

Committee Size

ESOP fiduciary and administrative committees are typically small, usually two to five non-ESOP shareholders and/or senior managers. The size of the committee reflects the technical nature of its responsibilities and decisions and the need to have members with appropriate knowledge who are able to understand and bear the fiduciary risk. In union companies where the union is actively involved with ESOP issues, the ESOP committee may include labor representatives, and the size of the committee may increase accordingly. Still, large ESOP fiduciary and administrative committees (more than eight members) are extremely rare in our experience.

Membership Qualifications

This type of committee requires members who can understand and fulfill their complex legal roles. Fiduciary committee members need to understand that their role is to represent and act in the exclusive best interests of ESOP participants as a whole—and not to represent the narrower interests of their various "constituents," (e.g. management, employees, or bargaining unit members). This aspect of the fiduciary committee's duties is not negotiable because it is a function of the underlying ERISA legal framework.

Many companies choose to restrict membership on the ESOP fiduciary/administrative committee to senior management. Other companies seek to involve nonmanagement employee-owners in what they believe is the "real ESOP decision-making," and these companies may include nonmanagers on the committee. In either case, companies should provide clear direction and education to committee members about their legal duties and responsibilities, both initially and on an ongoing basis. Failure to do so can not only result in an ineffective committee but also expose the ESOP and the company to significant legal risk. The good news is that the ESOP community is providing more in-depth resources for fiduciary/administrative committee members and trustees to learn about their duties and how to fulfill them effectively.

Membership Selection

The company's board of directors usually selects ESOP fiduciary/administrative committee members, based on the individuals best suited for the role. ESOP fiduciary/administrative committees are not meant to be representative bodies.

Communications Committees

Committee Size

Communications committees typically have 8 to 12 members. There are no legal requirements on committee size, but committees should be large enough to represent the different perspectives in the company, and small enough to permit individual members to contribute meaningfully in meetings. With fewer than 8 members, committees can fail to recognize the concerns of a broad range of employee-owners. With more than 12 regularly attending members, committees can easily become unwieldy. These are rules of thumb, however, not hard and fast principles. Some companies have managed successful committees with more members, by using subcommittees or other structures, or with smaller committees of 4 to 6 members.

In smaller companies, with a few hundred employees and only a few locations, a single ESOP committee may be sufficient, provided that its members represent a broad range of employees. In larger companies, with thousands or tens of thousands of employee-owners and/or many different locations, a cascading structure may be more appropriate. This means that individual operating divisions, plants, or profit centers may have their own local committees that work on local issues, and the company as a whole may have a top-level steering committee to coordinate on cross-divisional and company-wide ESOP issues. In companies with unions, the entire structure may be negotiated and become subject to the collective bargaining agreement.

Broad Representation

Most committees benefit from a "diagonal cross-section" of the workforce. Its members represent many different experience groups within the firm—different locations, seniority levels, professional and/or job classifications, race and gender diversity, and so on.

The cross-sectional representation captures the various experiences and perspectives that exist within the firm so the ESOP committee has access to the broadest range of thinking. Secondly, it also builds the credibility of the ESOP committee because employee-owners feel represented by their peers.

Many companies wrestle with whether to include senior management on the committee. It is critical that senior management demonstrate a commitment to the goals of the committee. In most companies, this is best served by having at least one senior manager serve directly on the committee, to provide legitimacy, give immediate feedback, and report back to the management team. Senior managers should, however, carefully avoid any tendency to take over. Effective senior management support is a delicate balancing act. An excess in either direction—too strong a management presence, or not strong enough—has crippled many ESOP committees.

Effective Mix of Skills

Committees must have members who are capable of doing its core work—either members already have these skills or are able to develop them. These skills may include managing team dynamics, facilitating meetings, managing projects, understanding the ESOP, understanding the business, working effectively with senior leadership, communicating well with peers, delivering trainings and presentations, and designing newsletters and other print and/or electronic publications. The specific skills required depend on the committee's goals and responsibilities. Failing to ensure that the committee as a whole has the necessary skills to complete its core tasks can result in committee ineffectiveness.

Some skills can be learned relatively easily, provided that at least someone on the committee already has the skills. These include running effective meetings, and project planning and monitoring. Other skills require more baseline capability and/or involved development. For example, a committee whose primary purpose is to communicate what the ESOP is and how it works will need to have members with effective writing and stand-up training skills.

Committees should also have an "internal learning" agenda, i.e. a plan to develop the skills and knowledge of its own members. (This is different from the "external training" agenda, i.e. the efforts of the committee to provide training to the rest of the company.) In other words, committees should have a plan to educate new members to get them up to speed and to keep all members learning on an ongoing basis. In some cases, ESOP committees have adopted a strategy of "certifying" their members. Certification may be structured so that it must be completed either before or after members are eligible to serve on the ESOP committee.

Membership Selection

There are many methods for selecting ESOP committee members. Some ESOP committees have members who are selected by senior leaders, while others have direct elections. Still others use some hybrid selection process, including nomination from the workforce and final selection by leadership, or vice versa. In companies in which the union is actively participating in the ESOP, the selection process is generally divided such that bargaining unit members pick their own representatives and nonbargaining unit employees pick theirs. Most ESOP communications committees have a selection process that involves some combination of direct voting and appointments.

Selecting the ESOP committee members provides an important opportunity for employee-owners to have "democratic" input and builds credibility. However, direct elections with no prior skill qualification or skill development plan can potentially undermine the committee's capacity. In the extreme, this may lead some to assume that because the committee is ineffective, democratic input does not work well.

The selection process should incorporate some mechanism to ensure that committee members have the required skills. A company can develop criteria and then solicit nominations that are restricted to individuals who meet the criteria. This "prequalification" ensures that only qualified employees are eligible to run in the first place, and allows the rest of the process to be more democratic. The final selections can be made either by senior leadership, by the committee itself, or by open elections (again, limited to the qualified nominees). Open elections create a greater sense of fairness and openness, while selection by leadership or the committee from among a slate of qualified nominees provides more control in ensuring the strongest overall final committee composition.

Member selection procedures often evolve over time. Many companies begin by appointing all (or at least many) of the initial ESOP committee members, to guarantee a good mix of skills and voices at the beginning. Over time, as old members rotate off the committee, those slots can be filled by elected representatives who meet whatever criteria have been developed.

Committee Decision-Making Processes

ESOP committees make different kinds of decisions, and the decision-making processes should match the type of decision being made. The formal decision-making process may be specified in the charter, or the committee may experiment and let it evolve.

Examples of decision-making processes include the consensus of all members, a final determination by the committee chair, weighted voting to give larger divisions and/or locations a larger voice (if they are not already represented by more committee members), and many others. As in all effective committees, clarity about the decision-making process is important to the accomplishment of committee goals. It is essential that committee members understand the decision-making processes and their limitations.

In practical terms, many committee decisions and recommendations are not controversial, once the committee has fully researched the question and considered its alternatives. In these cases, many committees do not feel the need to have a formal vote. The chair simply acknowledges that the decision has been reached. However, where there are strong feelings and differences of opinion that are not fully resolved after reasonable research, discussion, and debate, most committees find that voting is the fair way to reach a final decision or recommendation.

Committee Meetings

Committees should carefully consider what meeting schedule would be appropriate. The committee needs to meet often enough to accomplish its goals without creating an excessive burden. Some companies choose to have the committee meet monthly and review a standard agenda. This creates a regular process for reviewing progress toward completing committee activities, but the meetings can become stagnant unless committee members are making progress on the tasks.

Other committees schedule tasks and outcomes over the course of several months or a year, and committee members may manage their tasks independently and meet only when necessary. For instance, during the development of a specific training program, or when a newsletter is due, or in advance of a meeting to explain the ESOP participant statements, the committee (or a sub-team) may require significant meeting time to plan and coordinate the event. At other points, the committee may not meet at all. Committees that operate in this manner find it important to have a calendar or other scheduling tool to ensure that they reconvene with appropriate advance notice before each of their assigned tasks is due.

In addition to regular planning meetings or meetings around specific tasks and assignments, many committees have annual or biannual planning retreats, lasting usually one to two days. These planning retreats provide committee members more time to engage in team-building exercises, to evaluate and reflect on their work over the past year, to establish new goals, to generate and prioritize new ideas, and to draft a work plan for the upcoming year.

ESOP Committees Should Have Access to the Resources Necessary to Meet Their Goals

Communications Committees

Time

The primary resource that an ESOP committee needs is time, for committee members themselves and for other employees who participate in committee activities. The cost to the company depends on the range of activities. A few examples:

- *Employee ownership and business training.* These activities may require substantial time, both from the committee members (or a subcommittee) designing the training and then from employees attending training sessions.

- *Newsletters and other publications.* Preparing written documents (print or electronic) takes less time up front than designing training activities but requires an ongoing commitment that can add up in total time. The ESOP committee may take primary responsibility for these activities, or it may simply contribute ESOP-related content to other existing company communication initiatives.

- *Hotlines and frequently asked questions (FAQs).* Various committee-sponsored activities along these lines can require a significant investment of time to set up but less time to maintain. As employee-owners become more familiar with the ESOP over time, new questions will emerge, and the committee will need to update these resources.

- *Conferences.* Many committee members find that both attending regional and national conferences on ESOP-related issues and conducting company-to-company visits with other ESOP companies can help them tremendously with generating new ideas and learning from others' experiences. The cost for national conferences can be significant when travel and conference time, lodging, and registration fees are factored in. Local ESOP meetings and company visits can be more affordable in terms of both time and money.

- *General availability.* Committee members need time to manage ongoing mechanisms to solicit and respond to employees' questions about ownership and business issues. These may include committee "office hours," brown bag lunches, and regular update meetings. All of these efforts take place outside of the context of regular committee meetings.

ESOP committees function best when they have both specific objectives and time constraints. In this way, the committee is forced to prioritize its tasks to achieve its goals within its budget. As is often the case with committees and task forces, unlimited (or unstated) time budgets run the risk of encouraging the expansion of the tasks to fill the available time, with lost productivity. As with other committees, advance planning, goal-setting, and ongoing monitoring are the essential tools to ensure effective use of committee time and other company resources.

Access to Other Key Individuals Inside and Outside the Company

ESOP communications committees require regular interaction with other key individuals, depending on the issues that the committee is addressing. Early in its life cycle, the committee will require special access to key ESOP experts—either inside the company or the company's outside advisors—to build expertise on ESOP issues. Over time, most ESOP committees try to cultivate expertise in the committee itself, so that experienced members can train newer members. However, even mature ESOP committees benefit from and appreciate the opportunity to improve and refine their knowledge about the ESOP.

The committee may also need access to other individuals in different areas in the company. For example:

- *Senior management* can answer questions regarding company strategy and direction, and it should be actively involved in monitoring and evaluating the committee.
- *Human resources* can address questions regarding benefits and training.
- *Finance and administration* can address questions regarding the ESOP statement process, the connection between employee-owner actions and their impact on share value, and general business issues.
- *IT/MIS* can address and implement questions of intranet/internet communication and other technology issues. This support is critical for companies with geographically dispersed workforces and for committees that prefer to rely more on Web-based communications.

Money

An ESOP committee may spend money in several ways, depending on its objectives. ESOP committees may request funds to support various communication initiatives, such as print and/or electronic tools, or celebratory events. Committee members often attend local, regional, and national ESOP conferences, both to share their experiences and to learn from the experiences of other employee-owned companies.

Training to improve employee-owners' understanding of ownership, the ESOP, and/or the business can be one of the more costly activities undertaken by many ESOP committees. Some companies choose to assign the tasks of designing and conducting this type of training to the ESOP committee, while other companies assign these tasks to their human resources or other training groups. Additionally, a range of outside fee-based training opportunities in the ESOP market are specifically targeted to educating committee members and employee-owners. If one of the ESOP committees' core objectives is to educate employee-owners, then sufficient resources should be dedicated to develop internal ESOP training capabilities.

In summary, the ESOP committee will require access to a range of resources within the company, above and beyond the time of its members, to achieve its goals.

ESOP Committees Should Be Evaluated Regularly

ESOP Fiduciary/Administrative Committees

Evaluation for ESOP fiduciary/administrative committees consists primarily of periodic review by the board of directors to ensure that the committee is fulfilling its fiduciary and/or administrative duties. The fiduciary committee's decisions may also be subject to review by the U.S. Department of Labor (DOL), in the context of regular audits that the DOL performs of all ESOPs. The remainder of this section refers to ESOP communications committees.

Communications Committees

Communications committees, like all teams, require ongoing monitoring and evaluation. Over time, even committees that function very well early on will need to adapt to changing company circumstances. The most effective evaluation processes provide data to enable the committee to continuously improve its efforts. In support of this, ESOP committees should be evaluated on a 360-degree basis: by the employee-owners they serve, by senior leadership, and by the ESOP committee members themselves. This means that performance evaluation for the committee should be one of the tasks on the annual calendars of both the committee itself and of senior leadership.

Many ESOP committees have objectives that include long-term learning for employee-owners and performance improvements for the company. As with most evaluation, this presents a challenge: the committee's long-term goals may include things that are difficult to measure in the short run and that depend on the combined effort of the ESOP committee with other company efforts. Yet it is often not acceptable to wait many years to determine whether the committee's efforts are effective. Accordingly, ESOP committees may establish a series of short- and medium-term measures against which they can judge their progress and continually make adjustments to better reach their goals. As with any process improvement effort, there are different levels in the process, with shorter- to longer-term goals.

Process Review

The easiest thing to measure is whether the committee is conducting the activities that it committed to undertake in its work plan. Is it producing newsletters, conducting training sessions, answering employee-owners' questions, and/or completing other tasks on its work plan? If these "process" activities are occurring, and if senior leadership has reviewed the work plan, then both the committee and leadership will agree that "the right things are happening, and we should expect improved outcomes in the future."

As noted earlier, a new ESOP committee's first challenge is to identify its goals and then to establish a work plan to achieve them. As the committee develops, process evaluation consists of reviewing whether the committee has completed its work plan and determining whether members require further guidance or assistance to finish their agreed-upon tasks.

Outcome Review

Each activity should have targeted results that depend on the committee's core goals. For example, if a primary objective is to train employee-owners about how the ESOP works, then this second level of evaluation involves assessing whether employees who have been through the training have improved understanding. Some companies conduct rigorous testing, both quantitative and/or qualitative, while others rely on more intuitive measures, such as whether employee-owners "seem to be asking more of the right type of questions" or "appear to be paying attention to details better." Various survey tools are available for measuring these outcomes.[5] Intuitive measures are limited and can be quite misleading, but formal surveys can be time-consuming and expensive to design and administer.

Many companies build a brief assessment tool into each individual activity. These tools are most useful when they are designed to gather information on how the committee can improve its effectiveness.

For example:

- For training programs, presenters may ask participants to fill out brief "before-and-after" surveys covering a combination of technical and self-assessment questions.

- For newsletters, the committee may include a tear-off feedback form to get quick comments back from readers.

- For overall data, committee members may occasionally each interview a few (three to five) employees at random regarding the effectiveness of committee activities as a whole.

Impact Review

The final evaluation level assesses whether the committee is achieving its desired impact on the company. These longer-term measurements are the core success metrics that many companies seek to achieve with their ESOPs. If the ESOP committee's goals include improving understanding of the ESOP and of the business, do employee-owners in fact understand these issues better as a result of the committee's efforts? Does that understanding last beyond the week in which people attended the training? Has their behavior changed in ways that are contributing to business success? If the goals include improving specific operating performance measures, what is the effect on these measures over time?

It is possible that the ESOP committee can achieve its process and outcome objectives but still fail to contribute meaningfully to its impact objectives. In this case, it is essential for senior leadership

---

5.   The NCEO has comprehensive employee survey services available. In addition to questions that have been developed and tested over time, the NCEO also provides benchmarking data from other companies along with your results.

and the committee to reexamine the committee's goals and action plans to determine whether the goals are unrealistic, whether the action plans are not sufficiently focused on target impacts, or whether other factors external to the ESOP committee are interfering with achieving the desired impact.

It requires several years to see a significant impact, and the ESOP committee is only one component of a broader ownership culture development process. In the meantime, the interim measures of process and outcomes provide early indicators of whether the ESOP committee is completing its assigned tasks and whether the short- and mid-term outcomes are heading in the right direction.

Building Durable Committees

Communications Committees

Chapter 6 of this book discusses the life cycle of ESOP committees, but in the early days ESOP communications committees need to balance two competing needs: first, the need for new members to join the committee and learn how it functions, and second, the need to provide continuity so that the committee as a whole benefits from what its individual members have learned in the past.

These two needs can be met by establishing specific membership selection and rotation criteria. First, a certain number of committee slots should be reserved for employee-owners who have never served on the committee before, to ensure that new voices and perspectives are heard and to provide opportunities for different people across the organization to serve. Without these criteria, ESOP committees can become and/or become perceived as clubby and exclusive. This can also contribute to an "us-and-them" feeling among committee members, who may feel that they are the only ones working to ensure that the ESOP is successful.

The second criterion is that, after the first three to five years, a certain number of committee slots may be reserved for employee-owners who have served on the committee in the past in order to ensure continuity. Without this criterion, ESOP committees tend to cycle to entirely new members every few years, and they then need to reinvent the wheel each time. In the early years, all committee members are new, and there are few people who have served in the past. Committees tend to forget (or never recognize) the importance of history, and often fail to build a mechanism into their structure to recapture the experience of past committee members. Some structural mechanism for maintaining the experience level of the committee is essential, and designing this into the committee member selection criteria is an easy solution.

Dedicated, creative people are the committee's most critical resource. Over time, finding people to do the job may be challenging, especially after the initial enthusiasm for the ESOP is replaced by more "business as usual" attitudes. Lack of interest in serving often occurs in young ESOP committees, where employee-owners literally have no idea what the committee's potential can be, but it also happens in mature committees that have achieved past success but have run out of momentum.

Some companies are fortunate to have a steady flow of volunteers, but many need to charge management and/or committee members with a specific recruitment function. Potential new members can be invited as guests to a meeting, sent to conferences to meet committee members from other companies, or offered training in committee-related areas, such as financial education, as inducements.

Communications committees may also experience stagnation after the first few years of activity, which are often focused on ESOP education. As employee-owners become familiar with the ESOP, the communications committee may struggle with developing new and meaningful activities. Once again, regular contact with other companies' committees at conferences or other venues can provide members with new ideas. Evaluation of the committee's activities and discussion with senior leadership can identify new areas of focus and refine how the committee can best support the company's ownership objectives. Many committees find that over time, they shift their efforts from basic ESOP education to broader training on how the company's business works. Committees may also increase their role as a communications channel and focus more on gathering employee-owner input for leadership.

Conclusion

ESOP committees contribute meaningfully to a variety of company objectives. Some function as fiduciary committees, advising the ESOP trustee on a range of ESOP issues. Others function as communications committees, advising management (and labor, in union companies) on a range of communications and operational issues. The most successful ESOP committees have clear goals, full support and resources to achieve their goals, and effective evaluation mechanisms. These committees are an integral component of ESOP companies' broader efforts to engage employee-owners in improving company performance for the benefit of all shareholders.

CHAPTER 2

Duties of ESOP Administrative Committees

Corey Rosen and Loren Rodgers

Chapter 1 introduced the three primary types of ESOP committees: administrative committees (often called fiduciary committees), communications committees, and labor-management committees. This chapter focuses on the first type, and chapter 3 examines the second. This book does not cover labor-management committees in greater depth since they are less common than the other two types of ESOP committees. A single committee may fill both administrative and communication functions, but most companies separate the two types of committees.

An ESOP administrative committee is a group of people, usually appointed by the board of directors, that is delegated with the responsibility to oversee the day-to-day operations of the plan. It can be called different names, such as the plan administration committee or simply the ESOP committee. This book uses the term "ESOP administrative committee" to avoid confusion with the very different function of the ESOP communications committee.

All ESOPs must have a trustee and someone to administer the plan, but there is no legal requirement for there to be an ESOP administrative committee. In practice, however, plan documents almost always specify that there be an ESOP committee to administer the plan and oversee its operations. This chapter explores the roles and duties of ESOP administrative committees in a question-and-answer format.

Q. What is a fiduciary?

A. A plan fiduciary is a person or body that exercises any discretion-
ary authority or control over the management of the plan or the
assets of the plan or that provides investment advice to the plan
in return for compensation. Becoming a fiduciary is a weighty
decision, and no one should accept fiduciary responsibility until
they thoroughly understand the risks and responsibilities, and
the steps they must take to protect themselves and plan participants. Fiduciaries are held to high legal standards in making
decisions about the plan, and individual fiduciaries can be held
personally liable for losses suffered by the plan. In practice, law-
suits and government action against fiduciaries are rare, but the
potential for liability and the complexity of the rules governing
ESOPs mean that all fiduciaries must invest the time and care
to ensure that they make good decisions and document their
decision-making process.

Q. Is the ESOP administrative committee a plan fiduciary?

A. Possibly, but not necessarily. ESOPs have named fiduciaries,
which can be any individual or group (for example, the board,
the trustee, management, or all individual plan participants). The
ESOP administrative committee can be a named fiduciary, and
this will be clearly stated in your ESOP document. Even people
who are not named in the plan can still be fiduciaries. An ESOP
administrative committee may be considered a fiduciary, even if
not named as such in the plan document, if it makes decisions
for the operation of the plan or the plan's assets. Of course, the
other side of this issue is that the ESOP committee may not be
a fiduciary at all. For example, a committee that renders advice
to the fiduciary and/or trustee but does not exercise authority
over the plan would not be a fiduciary.

Q. Is the ESOP administrative committee the plan trustee?

A. Not usually. The committee can serve as the plan trustee, but
the two roles are usually separate.

Q. What are the typical areas of responsibility for ESOP administrative committees?

A. Administrative committees can have several responsibilities. They often assume responsibility for administrative oversight of the plan (making sure that statements are completed accurately and delivered in a timely fashion, that participants are paid, that allocations are properly made, and so on). Administrative committees themselves, however, rarely perform the actual work of plan administration, which is generally done by an outside administration firm with expertise in ESOPs. The committee may be responsible for plan design, including recommending amendments to the plan from time to time for adoption by the board of directors. In some cases, this could involve fiduciary issues, such as changing the plan in a way that reduces promised benefits to participants beyond what specific ESOP exceptions to ERISA allow. Some ESOP administrative committees make fiduciary decisions for the plan directly, and in other cases they may take fiduciary action indirectly by directing the trustee of the plan to make a decision. Remember, though, that some committees are not fiduciaries and simply act in an advisory role to the fiduciaries.

Q. What are typical activities of an administrative committee?

A. The list is a long one, but some of the key issues are:

- making sure that everyone who should be a participant in the plan actually is. In practice, this means ensuring that the plan administrator sets up accounts for everyone who has met the participation requirements;

- ensuring that every participant's account receives proper allocations, interest income, and forfeitures;

- making sure the administrator files the proper reports with the government, obtains the necessary forms for spousal consent, follows the plan's procedures for reinstating people into the plan who have left the company and returned, that qualified domestic relations orders are followed, and so on;

- guaranteeing that proper procedures are followed in the case of employee complaints about the plan and that other employee rights, such as voting and the opportunity to inspect plan documents, are provided;

- hiring and evaluating a plan administrator;

- hiring and evaluating an investment manager for non-stock assets in the plan;

- assuring that contributions to the plan are properly credited;

- making sure that participants who qualify for diversification receive proper notification and have the opportunity to make diversification elections;

- overseeing plan distributions to assure they are done properly;

- having a repurchase obligation study done and creating a plan to deal with the issue;

- interpreting plan provisions;

- adopting any additional rules that may be necessary to make specific what may be general plan provisions (e.g., plans sometime provide discretion to the ESOP committee about when to make certain distributions, provided the distributions are made in a nondiscriminatory way and are spelled out in written policy);

- responding to any errors discovered in the plan or its operation;

- providing the administrator with the information needed to operate the plan and getting from the administrator the information necessary to file tax reports; and

- keeping minutes of committee meetings.

This may sound like a daunting list, but in practice most of the work is done by the plan's administrator. However, the ESOP committee must make sure that the administrator is competent and must oversee its functioning.

Q. What are examples of fiduciary decisions the ESOP committee might make?

A. Fiduciary decisions include many of the issues listed above. Specifically, fiduciary decisions include, but are not limited to, deciding on the voting of ESOP-held shares where the law does not require a pass-through of voting rights to participants, making decisions about investing plan assets both in employer stock and in other investments, selling stock, ensuring that the ESOP pays no more than fair market value, selecting qualified advisors, assuring that the operation and design of the plan complies with ERISA, and moving assets from the ESOP to another plan. The committee may implement these decisions itself or direct the trustee to carry them out.

Q. What activities by an administrative committee are not fiduciary decisions?

A. Many activities are not fiduciary actions, including:

- the committee's normal administration of the plan, presuming that such administration is in compliance with the law;
- its voting for one person or another for the board of directors; and
- its recommendation to the board of directors to terminate the plan, change plan features within acceptable ERISA boundaries, or increase or decrease funding of the plan in a nonleveraged situation.

Q. What are the ESOP administrative committee's legal constraints in deciding how to vote or direct the tendering of ESOP shares?

A. Legally, the ESOP administrative committee must make any decision as to the voting or tendering of shares (other than those for which the plan provides a pass-through vote to participants) based on the best interests of plan participants as participants, not as employees. In other words, the committee (or any other fiduciary) cannot consider the employment interests of participants. Instead, the committee must look to the long-term value of the accounts in the plan. Many consultants argue that the committee may also consider the preservation of employee ownership as part of the legitimate interests of participants, provided this is spelled out as a plan purpose. The ESOP administrative committee cannot make a decision that is primarily for the benefit of other parties, such as management or other owners.

Even where the employees direct the voting or tendering of shares, however, there is disagreement on whether the ESOP committee (or other fiduciary) can simply follow these instructions, and, if so, when. Following participant directions is simple in most circumstances, but many experts argue that when the fiduciary believes the participants have directed a vote that is not in their best interests, the fiduciary has an obligation not to follow the direction.

Q. What is the role of an ESOP administrative committee in communicating the plan?

A. The only legal responsibility of the ESOP administrative committee in terms of plan communications is to make sure that participants receive a summary plan description, a summary of material modifications in the event of a plan amendment, a summary annual report, and appropriate reports on participants' account balances.

In practice, the ESOP committee may also be responsible for other communications to plan participants, such as simplified brochures describing the plan, coordinating employee ownership month activities, helping design and deliver information about company financials, developing videos, audio recordings, or other non-written material, coordinating employee orientations to the ESOP and periodic company meetings, and working on other activities designed to help people understand the plan and the company. In some companies, the ESOP committee also serves as the coordinating committee for employee involvement programs (work teams, suggestion systems, etc.). None of these things is legally required, but the most effective plans are those in which the employees have an active role in helping their colleagues understand how the ESOP works.

This book assumes that the activities described above are carried out by an ESOP communications committee instead of an administration committee, but it is possible that a single committee might serve both administrative and communications roles.

Q. How are ESOP administrative committee members chosen?

A. Since many of the functions of the committee are inherently duties of the board of directors that are delegated to the committee, most committees are appointed by the board. But, other than general legal and fiduciary concerns, there are no rules about who can be on the ESOP committee or how they should be selected. In many companies, the committee consists of members of management and/or the board; in some, it is just a single member of management. More participative companies get nonmanagement employees involved on the committee as minority or majority members. Usually these are elected by other employees, but sometimes they are appointed by management or are volunteers.

Q. How do companies prepare committee members?

A. There are no legal guidelines about the training, qualifications, or expertise required of members of an ESOP administrative committee. The duties are complex and the penalties for mistakes are large, so many companies extensively train potential committee members so that they can make informed choices about joining the committee. Some companies limit committee membership to people with relevant expertise. Other companies provide extensive training and educational resources for committee members. The training may include books, online training, and in-person meetings, all of which are available through the NCEO and other organizations. Others invite practitioners to educate committee members.

Q. How do companies minimize the risk to administrative committee members?

A. Proper education and training for committee members is essential. A proper understanding of the fiduciary responsibilities and risks of committee decisions should ensure the committee members are motivated to seek out and minimize potential sources of risk. Other solutions are to make sure that the committee has adequate time and resources. Committees that feel time pressure or feel an expectation that they will "rubber stamp" decisions made by the administrative firm or the company's senior leadership are less likely to fully investigate issues that they should. All ESOP companies should encourage committee members and other fiduciaries to network extensively with other ESOP companies and to attend conferences where they can learn and ask questions from experts. Finally, making careful decisions about the service providers you hire will ensure that they are competent, honest, and have sufficient experience with ESOPs to prevent problems with your plan.

CHAPTER 3

Activities of ESOP Communications Committees

Loren Rodgers

Because ESOP communication committees at different companies have different goals, budgets, levels of experience, and types of ESOPs, they vary widely from company to company. There are no universal guidelines or rules of thumb that will work in every company. This chapter's goal is to give you a sampling of ideas and examples of what ESOP communications committees actually do in successful ESOP companies.

Read this chapter with an open mind and, even if you do not find any specific activities to copy, you will develop an expanded sense of what an ESOP committee can do. Then innovate. Ask yourself, "Why shouldn't the committee take care of charitable giving?" Or, instead of charity, maybe the committee should handle office redesign, or the company wellness program, or the cultural integration of a recently acquired company. It could create an employee survey or an educational game. It could orchestrate a community celebration or a visit to your member of Congress. Embrace large dreams for your ESOP committee, and see where the committee takes them.

Foster Innovation

Walman Optical established its ESOP in 1989 and has about 900 employees in 40 locations. The company, which provides diverse products and services to the optical industry, set up an innovation committee to make some concrete changes in the company operations to save money and reduce resource use. The goal was to reduce energy use by 20% and switch 30% of energy to renewable fuels. The committee split into three teams, each focusing on a different area (trash, recycling, water and sewer; packaging; and shipping and delivery). The teams used a systematic process to brainstorm and prioritize ideas, and ended up finding multiple solutions. Many were simple, such as putting recycling bins in locations that did not have them. That cut trash volume by 50%. Repairing leaking fixtures cut the water bill by 90% in one location. These easy changes created a 20% year-on-year savings in packaging materials and reduced shipping expenses by $240,000 in 2009.

Develop an Elite Team

Building Materials Distributors, a 100% ESOP-owned company based in Galt, California, created an Employee Ownership Advisory Team, a permanent team that provides in-depth education about the ESOP and general business concepts to a small group of employees. These employees then become in-house trainers and communicators about the ESOP and financial information for other employees. The training lasts for two years, and the team consists of five employees, one from each department: a driver, sales representative, computer clerk, accounting person, and warehouse employee. All employees vote for who will serve on this team.

The president, corporate controller, and human resources director conduct the training. The team meets once a month for a four-hour session. The HR director coordinates training topics and speakers. The training focuses on employee understanding of and communications about the ESOP. They also learn about financial statements, ESOP administration, how to interpret the ESOP statement, high-involvement management, and the ownership cultures of other ESOP companies. Once employees complete the training, they become "certified employee owners" (CEOs) and receive a $500 cash bonus.

The members of the team then serve as trainers for communicating ESOP understanding to other employees. They also participate in the quarterly employee meetings by assisting in the explanation of financial information and how to interpret the ESOP statement.

These CEOs become ideal candidates for the ESOP Employee Committee, a group that facilitates communication between employees, management, ESOP trustees, and the board of directors. This group meets biweekly and is composed of elected non-management employees, one from each department.

Other companies manage CEO programs with less formal structure and time commitment than BMD. They may require five two-hour courses, for example, or passing a series of quizzes. Companies often distribute certificates to all CEOs, and some hang a picture of each CEO in a prominent place in the company's main office.

Add ESOP Content to an Intranet Site

Some committees set up an ESOP-focused zone on the company's intranet (internal Web site). The site can provide easy access to basic plan documents (like the summary plan description), current statistics about the ESOP (the latest valuation or number of participants), calculators (if I joined on date X and worked full time, what percentage vested is my account?), and much more. Some committees host a game (guess the stock price). Others may include video interviews with current or former participants, or a message from the CEO about the value of the ESOP. Companies that do an employee survey may post the results on their intranet site, and others may have a virtual suggestion box.

Help with the ESOP Rollout

Many ESOP communications committees get their start with the initial announcement of the plan to participants. The committee may be formed in order to help design and present some of the core content during the rollout, or to follow up the rollout with a small-group presentation designed to reinforce and extend the lessons of the rollout.

Educate Yourselves

One of the most effective ESOP committees in the country is at Van Meter. The case study chapter in this book covers some of the ways

Van Meter's committee has been so effective, but one in particular may not be obvious. For the first half-year it existed, the committee did just about nothing that was visible to anyone outside the committee itself. Committee members spent time thoroughly educating themselves about their ESOP and how it works. They worked through all the nuts and bolts of participation, vesting, allocation, diversification, and distribution using hypothetical employees, they went to seminars, and they quizzed ESOP experts. It was only after they created this solid foundation for themselves that the committee began serious efforts at education and building awareness.

Create Educational Games

The range of educational games used by ESOP committees is huge. One of the simplest fun-based incentive systems is an idea created by SRC Holdings (formerly named Springfield ReManufacturing Company) called "mini-games." In fact the company set up a consulting group called the "Great Game of Business" to teach others how to use mini-games. In their booklet "Get in the Game," the Great Game of Business staff defines a mini-game as a time-specific program to meet an operational goal. The goals are set through the involvement of the employees involved. Targets could include billable hours, new customers, product yield, average collection days, inventory accuracy, customer satisfaction, on-time delivery, calls per hour, or just about any other measure that is important to a business.

Employees then set goals, often publishing them for other teams to see. Typical time frames are one to a few months. A scorecard is posted so everyone can track progress. The information should be sufficient to provide details needed for action, but not so detailed as to be hard to review in a minute or two. The charts often are graphic. Rewards do not need to be economically significant. They can be feel-good prizes, like tickets to a game or dinner; a recognition award, such as a trophy; a fun award, such as a gift certificate or lottery tickets; or anything else the team decides will have meaning. The games also need to address a real problem (don't just play to play) and have realistic goals, understandable rules, and a short enough time period to sustain interest.

At Pool Covers, for instance, employees help set goals for specific targets, such as service call-backs. Employee teams were created (sales, office, and field staff) and each was asked to come up with a set of goals, such as increasing sales, improving the billable hours percentage, shop time for a pool cover repair, or getting staff into the field with fewer errors. If the goals were met, everyone got a bonus.

Broadcast a Fact of the Day

CALIBRE is a management and technology services company. Based in Alexandria, Virginia, the company was founded in 1989 and established an ESOP in 1994. For employee ownership month in 2006, CALIBRE's Employee Owners Advisory Committee (EOAC) sent out an email "fact of the day." Examples included:

- "Your BOD-directed ESOP contribution this past year was 7.25%. That doesn't even include the 40.8% you earned on existing shares."
- "Over half of CALIBRE's employees are 100% vested in their ESOP accounts."
- "The value of your ESOP account changes only once a year, when the stock valuation occurs."
- "A 'leveraged ESOP' is one that funds the purchase of stock with borrowed money."

Have a Role in Governance

At CALIBRE, the EOAC elects one of its five members to serve on the company's board of directors.

Roll with the Changes

Phelps County Bank (PCB) is an ESOP-owned bank in Rollo, Missouri, and one of the most-imitated companies in employee ownership. In the early days of its ownership culture, PCB used something it called a "problem buster" committee. Management selected a cross-section of employees for the committee, which solicited ideas or problems (employees didn't have to have a solution) from other employees. The committee would circulate these ideas to other employees, get feedback, and conduct its own review. It could then either make a decision or make a recommendation to management, depending on the kind of issue involved. Employees submitting an idea or problem had to sign off on its final resolution or it came back for further review.

Over time, however, the system worked so well it eventually no longer fit the company: employees became accustomed to simply identifying and solving problems on their own or in informal groups, and the problem-buster committee was disbanded in favor of self-managing work teams. These teams brought the company to a higher level of employee involvement—one where involvement is fundamentally structured into each employee's day-to-day job, but in time, this participation structure stopped fitting the company as well. Today, PCB has a new participation structure: people now participate in functional teams, such as a technology services committee. The new system is not necessarily more or less involvement-focused than either of the old systems, but different. At PCB, employee involvement changes with the times and company conditions.

Design and Implement Communication

One of the most powerful ways to develop and continually revise an educational program about ownership is to get employee-owners involved. At PCB, for example, a committee of employees is in charge of developing communications about the ESOP. The committee is composed of six employees and an alternate, all of whom are elected by the staff. The chairman must be a nonmanagement employee. The committee does whatever it can to promote knowledge of the ESOP, such as putting together a monthly newsletter called "ESOP Pride," conducting ESOP orientation for new employees, and constantly trying to generate new ideas to communicate to people. One idea the committee generated was the "ESOP Challenge," which provided a monthly $100 prize for the best suggestion or idea submitted to the committee that month. The idea had to be thoroughly researched and documented with respect to cost, time line, method of implementation, and potential benefits. At the end of the year, the committee held a random drawing of all the ideas submitted for a $1,500 prize.

At MPD, an Owensboro, Kentucky-based ESOP company with several hundred employees, a "Participants' Committee" is in charge of facilitating education about the ESOP. This committee has ten members, one who is appointed by management and acts as chair, as well as nine others, who are elected by all employees. The group of nine includes three hourly, three nonexempt, and three exempt employees. Like PCB, the committee produces an ESOP newsletter, which is published 25 to 30 times each year, conducts new employee orientations, and generates new ideas for communication. The committee developed MPD's monthly brown-bag lunches as a forum for discussing financial information on a regular basis. The CEO presides over these lunches, which feature reports from management and nonmanagement employees. Although attendance is voluntary, the average has been around 70% of the staff. To increase attendance, everyone who attends is eligible to receive a door prize of $75. It may not seem like much, but who would not want to go to lunch and come back with $75 in his or her pocket?

Run an Employee Orientation Program

At Bimba Manufacturing, a 500-employee company that is 90% owned by the ESOP, the ESOP committee has put together an orientation process based on the method developed at another employee ownership company, Web Industries. Orientation takes 20 hours over a two-week period and includes meeting with the company president to discuss the corporate philosophy and goals, meeting with all the company officers, a one-hour team meeting each day during the first 20 days of employment, and classes. The classes are taught by employee volunteers, and topics include company history, open-book management, teamwork, work ethics, problem recognition and solving, and the ESOP, among many others. Employees are oriented not only to the job, the company, and the ESOP, but also to the culture.

One theme of these successful committees is that they cultivated creative ideas that had the potential to fail. Innovation happens when people make space for it, so if your committee is stuck, then maybe the time has come to step back and set aside some time for creative thinking. Dream a bit about what the committee might be able to accomplish, then see where those dreams take you.

Part 2
Best Practices

Developing an Effective ESOP Communications Committee

Jim Bado

If you want to communicate your ESOP's benefits, a strong, focused ESOP communications committee can be an invaluable tool. Unfortunately, as many companies have discovered, the road to building an effective ESOP communications committee is littered with potholes. Progress is shattered by common developmental mistakes such as having no clear mission, lacking management support, losing credibility, failing to connect the committee's mission to business goals, and establishing unrealistic expectations.

The good news is a small investment in proper planning up front will prevent big performance problems down the road. You can, to paraphrase Thomas Carlyle, turn the obstacles in your path into stepping stones. Whether you're just starting your committee or working to reinvigorate your present team, following the field-tested cycle explained in this chapter will help ensure your committee's success.

Step 1: Design and Formation

Before you create an ESOP communications committee, ask yourself: Why do you want it? What do you envision it accomplishing? What will it be doing in five years?

If you cannot think of concrete, specific answers, then save the money, time, and energy you're planning to invest and spend it on something more worthwhile. If you decide to move forward, your first step is addressing the basic design issues. Some are pretty clear and some aren't, like:

- Who is on the committee?
- How are they selected?
- Will there be terms?
- Will the committee have a budget?

Ideally, the committee should include a variety of job functions—such as production, warehouse, office staff, and sales—and be representative of your company in terms of race, gender, ethnicity, and seniority. For example, the Chilcote Company in Cleveland has reflected its diverse workforce by having Slavic, African-American, Lebanese, and Chinese members on its committee.

By including individuals from diverse backgrounds, committee members can tailor their activities to different audiences, greatly improving their effectiveness. Effective peer-to-peer communication means that someone I perceive as my peer is communicating to me. Even if your company does not have language or cultural barriers, you'll want a diverse group. A customer-service rep and an engineer, for example, do not see things the same way. Having them on the committee both improves communication and tears down the "silo" mentality that exists among departments in most companies.

Another membership consideration is whether you want to have a management liaison. Some firms think this is critical to success, like LeFiell Manufacturing in California, which has had a management representative on its committee from day one. Some ESOP companies prefer to have the committee composed entirely of nonmanagers, and others mix nonmanagers, supervisors, and managers on their committee. Careful consideration of your company's culture, the role the ESOP communications committee will have, and your goals for the committee will help you decide on its composition.

At a company with multiple locations, it is a definite plus to have representatives from the different facilities. Parametrix, a multi-location engineering ESOP, selects members from any office with more than 15 employees. Other multi-location ESOPs follow this model. A company with multiple locations or divisions can delegate the member-selection process to the leadership of each division, empowering them to make the decision. Delegating the selection process will help ensure that local leadership supports the efforts of the committee.

There are many ways to choose committee members. Scot Forge Company in Spring Grove, Illinois, elects its entire nine-member committee to staggered terms. Proactive companies define clear criteria for their ESOP communications committees. Albums Inc, a distributor headquartered in Strongsville, Ohio, created a series of concrete criteria for committee members. It appoints its committee after self-nominated candidates go through a 20-minute interview with an outside ESOP consultant, who makes recommendations based on which candidates will strengthen the current committee.

The salient design points are to structure your committee and to implement a selection process that reinforces your corporate culture, addressing any challenges or issues that you've encountered with previous team efforts. As with any ongoing internal communications initiative, it is essential that upper- and mid-level leaders view the ESOP communications committee as an entity that will complement their communications efforts. Lack of leadership support, whether overt or covert, has hamstrung many ESOP communications committees' efforts. Take the time to cultivate it. Too many committees have crashed because leadership support was weak.

It is also critical from the outset to recognize the ESOP communications committee as a long-term investment in developing ownership skills and knowledge. Like any effective team, the committee needs time to gel and to sort out its new role. (See chapter 6 for an in-depth look at this issue.) The Braas Company—a pioneer in ESOP communications committee development—estimates that it took its committee almost two years of education and training before it could accomplish anything substantial (a case study of Braas is in chapter 9). While following a game plan will accelerate this process, if you see the committee as a short-term fix rather than as part of your firm's long-term evolution, you may want to rethink whether you are ready for a committee.

Step 2: Define Mission and Goals

Once the committee is formed with the appropriate mix of employees, its first task is defining its mission and goals. Committee members need to go through this process together. Some committees may want to educate themselves about their ESOP prior to taking this step—and that is fine—but they need to do this before committing to projects.

At this juncture, it is important to stop the committee from simply jumping into action, without first providing some direction. Otherwise, the committee may have some early success, but that success will be short-term. A mission and clear goals point the committee in the right direction for the long term, helping it steer clear of areas outside its focus. Without direction, committees can drift into issues beyond their expertise and authority (e.g., personnel matters), which in turn erodes management support.

To avoid "issue drift" management needs to set the general parameters for the committee, making sure that the committee's purpose is in alignment with the business's goals and objectives. Management's task is akin to defining the playing field. Once that is done, managers need to back off and let the committee flesh out its vision within those parameters.

In figuring out their mission and goals, ESOP committee members ought to ask themselves questions like:

- Why do we exist?

- Who do we serve?

- What products or services do we provide?

The process of developing a mission and goals is often more critical than what is finally on paper in the end. Through the mission development process, ESOP communications committee members define what they are and—maybe even more importantly—what they are not. At Westfield Tanning, in Westfield, Pennsylvania, working with an outside facilitator taught committee members, according to one member, Bill Reed, "how to develop a mission; how to plan for the present and the future; and how to communicate with the rest of the workforce, managers, and staff." Before taking the time to develop a mission, Reed notes that committee members were frustrated with their role and almost ready to give up. Defining a mission focused the committee on educating employees to support Westfield Tanning's objective of having people act like owners.

To strengthen the process, the final mission and goals should be approved by management and commented on by employee-owners. Management review will help ensure support of the ESOP communications committee's efforts as will comments by employees, who are ultimately the committee's customers. Committees solidify their mission and goals by inserting them into the group's bylaws; successful committees review and revise them on at least an annual basis. An ESOP committee's mission and goals should be living documents to guide the team and help it achieve its purpose, not something put in a frame, hung on the wall, and forgotten.

Investing time in mission development will help the committee avoid unrealistic expectations and the inevitable disappointment stemming from its failure to meet lofty goals. "Don't set your expectations too high, so they do not meet reality. Yet set them high enough to achieve growth and education for all," comments Mike Palitto of Reuther Mold's ESOP communications committee. "You need to have a lot of patience with those who do not know as much about your ESOP as you may."

Step 3: Committee Member Education

Once the committee decides where it's going, members need to educate themselves. There are three areas in which committee members should become knowledgeable: technical (the facts), presentation (conveying the facts) and process (how the committee functions).

Technical Knowledge

On the technical side, committee members need to build a practical, layman's understanding of your ESOP plan. If members are going to communicate about your business—as many committees do—they need a basic financial understanding also. Technical education can start with the summary plan description and the ESOP rules. Many companies have gone though the summary plan line by line, page by page. Education, of course, ought not end with the summary plan. Issues like the stock valuation process, repurchase obligation, the ESOP trustee's role, and a rudimentary knowledge of tax law are helpful in addressing employees' questions.

It takes time to build in-depth knowledge, so exposing ESOP communications committee members to multiple sources of information and lots of repetition is beneficial. There are a plethora of conferences and events sponsored by the NCEO, the ESOP Association, and the Foundation for Enterprise Development (FED) that committee members can attend. Scot Forge sends its ESOP council members to local and national ESOP conferences. "Every year two to four council members have attended these educational seminars and returned with new ideas to share with employee-owners," commented council member Jamie Kirk. Taking the next step and serving on an outside organization's board or committees can provide committee members with a new perspective on employee ownership and better networking opportunities.

Other ESOP communications committees build reference libraries and, like Web Industries, have reading circles where they discuss important books. Committees have also gained new ideas by visiting local ESOPs and arranging "ESOP exchange" programs. Others, like O'Neil & Associates, have hosted events for their local ESOP Association chapters. You learn more about your company and your ESOP when you have to explain it to someone else.

Conferences, books, and visits are good, but in the end, committee members need to know about their own ESOP and how to explain it to the rest of the workforce. Many companies bring in outsiders who are well versed in ESOP knowledge and can explain its complexities to committee members in layman's terms. Firms may use their lawyers, lenders, administrators, and appraisers to educate their committees. There, however, is wide variation among professionals in the ability to translate their technical expertise into easily understood terms.

To compensate, many firms use training and development specialists as well. The most successful committees know that making learning fun and engaging is essential to their effectiveness. Using a hands-on learning tool (such as an ESOP game) accelerates learning and enables committee members to anticipate their peers' questions and to use a simple visual model to provide answers. In addition, ongoing education from insiders can also be a great educational source for committee members. The key is training and education specifically focused on your ESOP, not a generic course on employee ownership.

Presentation Skills

The second area of a committee member's education is building the skills to explain the ESOP to another person. This goes well beyond technical knowledge. At Northwest Swissmatic in Minnesota, the ESOP communications committee went through a train-the-trainer process to build the skills to explain their ESOP and business in layman's terms. Other firms have taken the trainer development process a step further with quarterly classes where committee members educate their peers on the ESOP, the company's financials, and its business strategy. At some of these firms, for example, classes have included topics such as an overview of the competition.

Team Process Skills

On a process level, the third area, committee members must learn how to work together. They are a team, and they need to function like one. At many companies, in fact, they are the model for teams throughout the company—the committee is composed of the firm's best and brightest working together to support the ESOP. Developing a working knowledge of how to run an effective meeting, the roles people play in groups, team dynamics, and how to take minutes and parcel out assignments will facilitate the committee's effectiveness. The committee needs to have a chair, either elected or appointed, to ensure that someone is responsible for keeping it alive and moving forward on its tasks. An experienced facilitator, whether a company insider or an outsider, also improves team effectiveness. Providing help with meeting skills up front will eliminate team-development challenges and accelerate the committee's progress.

Step 4: Action

Once the mission is in place and committee members are comfortably educated, the committee can revisit its goals and decide how to take action. There are many good ways to do this. Committees that are just beginning ought to think about taking on a project that is easy to accomplish and will give the committee maximum positive exposure with employees. Remember that the committee is still building credibility with employees. At Chilcote, the committee organized a company open-house and then ran the firm's annual presentation of its ESOP certificates, explaining the certificate to employees in 30- to 45-minute presentations punctuated by questions and answers.

Other firms, like Braas, have taken years to create highly evolved ongoing educational processes. Braas' CEO certified employee-owner, or "CEO" program (formerly called ESOP Buddies™) is run by its employee ownership committee to teach people practical knowledge and skills in four areas: the ESOP, company financials, stock valuation, and company culture. Braas' committee uses a customized handbook to teach sessions during lunch, before or after work, and on company time. ESOP committee members "buddy up" with employees, taking them through the educational process. Employees graduate by earning their CEO status and receive public recognition.

Many ESOP communications committees develop employee orientation programs for both the ESOP and the company. At O'Neil & Associates, the ESOP committee holds an orientation session where it uses a customized PowerPoint presentation to educate new employees about the ESOP's benefits. As a "take home," participants are given the company's simplified summary plan description. Parametrix's committee's orientation program has four tenets: (1) keep it simple, (2) focus on a feeling of ownership philosophy, (3) welcome ESOP participants when they qualify for the plan, and (4) repeat, repeat, repeat.

No matter what projects they take on—from ownership education and facilitating the election of a new board member to holding an "ESOP Olympics" and burying an ESOP time capsule—an effective committee ends up doing some things that are educational; some that are promotional (both inside and outside the company); and some that are just plain fun, like ESOP week activities, cookouts, watermelon day, and picnics. The important thing, again, is to see all these events as part of an ongoing strategy to build an ownership culture at your company. And to make sure the committee is focusing its energy on things within its control and sphere of influence. Developing an ownership mentality, where employees act like business people, is not a one-time thing; it is more like a marathon than a sprint.

Step 5: Evaluation

In the end, you've got to go back to the beginning. Effective teams—whether or not they are ESOP communications committees—spend time evaluating their projects. They ask questions like: Did we meet our objectives? Did the project move us toward accomplishing our mission? What went well and what did not? Many committees drop the ball on evaluation, losing an opportunity to congratulate themselves, improve their effectiveness, and provide closure.

Some firms conduct formal surveys to see how they are doing or to set a baseline to target their efforts prior to taking action. However it is accomplished, effective evaluation leads back to the committee's mission and goals and encourages the committee to re-examine these in light of what it has accomplished.

Part of the evaluation process ought to be succession planning (yes, this affects ESOP committees too). Creating set terms at the beginning facilitates succession planning and helps ensure joining the committee isn't a "life sentence." Designing a membership process with staggered terms will continuously bring new employees and new ideas to the team. Committee members also need to plan for how new leaders will be selected. Having a co-chair can ensure a smooth transition. When the chair finishes his or her term, the co-chair becomes the new chair and the committee selects a new co-chair.

Following the steps outlined in this chapter will help to ensure your ESOP communications committee's success. By investing time up front, you'll steer clear of the potholes and build a core group of dedicated, committed owners. You will also develop a committee whose members understand the benefits of the ESOP, take "ownership" of ESOP communications, and help their peers to think and act like business people.

CHAPTER 5

Leadership and ESOP Committees

Jack Veale

ESOP committees exist in many forms and with different functions, responsibilities, and membership. The previous chapters of this book discuss the types of ESOP committees, how they work, and what some best practices are. This chapter is about leadership of the company and the ESOP committee, because in most cases, the two are intertwined. The starting point in this chapter is the company culture because it affects the success and leadership of the ESOP committee.

How a Company's Culture Affects an ESOP Committee

In many presentations to ESOP companies, I have asked, "Please raise your hand if you have raised children, and you have nieces and nephews who were raised and behave the same way as your children." With very few exceptions, no hands are raised. Some look around and laugh or smile when they see the result. The lesson of this exercise is that families with brothers and sisters don't raise their children the same way or with the same outcomes. Neither do ESOP companies!

Each leadership team has its own way of communicating, engaging, and supporting its organization. One ESOP company's culture cannot simply be applied to another company. Leadership, governance, and ownership expectations vary from person to person and company to company. If the company hired a new vice president of sales who is not involved in the committee and lacks an appreciation for the ESOP, he or she will affect the committee's effectiveness. ESOP committees should listen and learn how other ESOP companies have their ESOP committees create excitement. However, you should not expect to always have the same results, because your company may not have the culture to embrace those activities, just as different families raise children different ways in different circumstances. An ESOP culture can be defined as the company's distinctive and unique set of behaviors that engage the organization to improve enterprise value and sustainability for the future. This is not "touchy-feely" stuff. I am not a therapist; I am an MBA and a former CFO of a high-growth $100 million company. My approach for leading an ESOP committee does not involve "kumbaya" activities. It is about getting results.

Having a meeting without achieving a result or making a decision is a waste of time. Have you attended a meeting in the last year where the discussions had no end, no decision, no clarity of direction, and no buy-in among the committee's members? When I ask audiences this question, 90%–100% of them raise their hands. Your company's culture affects whether such unproductive meetings occur, and your ESOP committee must deal with the problem. However, you can remedy this situation through effective leadership. Consider the four concepts below as measures of a company's culture:

1. *Produce results:* Does the organization have plans and goals with measureable milestones and activities? This measures the company's effectiveness in developing growth.

2. *Administer (or control):* Does the organization have systems, policies, and procedures to control the quality and reduce errors and mistakes? This measures the company's efficiency in achieving profitability.

3. *Entrepreneur (or innovation and risk-taking):* Does the management team allow experimentation and piloting activities that create new or better products, allow leadership development through major projects, and achieve long-term effectiveness? This measures management's willingness to change, ability to take risks, and encourage leadership deep in the organization.

4. *Integration:* Does the organization empower people using teams, or is the organization hierarchal, using a top-down management style? This measures the organization's ability to respond to marketplace threats, develop a deep leadership bench, and improve execution more efficiently with speed and few mistakes.

If you are a partially unionized manufacturing company with one location that implemented an ESOP 30 years ago, your culture will be very different from an engineering firm with multiple locations that recently implemented an ESOP and is still majority-owned by the company founder. In both cases, people may be relatively happy, involved with the growth of the company, and enjoying increasing stock prices. Similarly, there may be two companies, both nonunion, that are competing in the same marketplace (such as government staffing services), only in different locations. The two may have different and unique ownership cultures that still produce results. While an ESOP committee's effectiveness will be influenced by the organization's culture, any committee can increase its effectiveness by following a few simple principles.

Leading an ESOP Committee

Who leads? There are three basic models of ESOP committee leadership:

1. In a command-and-control environment, the CEO or a senior executive is the chair of the committee. The chair drives the agenda, and members of the committee are assigned tasks by the chair and follow his or her lead unconditionally.

2. In an organization with an engaged management style, the chair of the committee is often a senior executive or key manager, like the CFO or vice president of human resources, and others below are assigned to the committee to be groomed for broader knowledge of the company and to improve their leadership capacity.

3. Finally, the chair of an empowered committee may be an elected position where some or all of the members are elected by the employees following a rigorous and transparent selection process.

All of these models are very effective when they fit the culture of the company. Of course, there are hybrids of these three models, and in most cases they are found in successful ESOP committees at successful companies.

If you are a senior executive or CEO serving as the committee chair, make sure you have a plan for getting your committee to work when you are not present. In many cases, your leadership style may be stifling and controlling, so new ideas will not surface. Leaders with top-down leadership styles tend to be blind to their behavior and to how others respond in front of them. To outsiders, it can be startling. If you want to engage people for a higher purpose, make sure you are willing to listen to the lower-level people on the team. Limit your tenure as chair and pass the baton to others in the committee. Defining your exit will show support for the committee and will encourage others to step up and replace you.

As the committee evolves away from the having the CEO or senior executive as the chair, the former leading executive should become the sponsor of the committee and help the new leader learn to lead. As the new chair evolves into a successful leader, the committee usually becomes a self-managing, empowered team of cross-functional performers who execute activities to support the ESOP and its ownership culture.

ESOP Committee Best Practices

Charter and Budget

The committee charter is similar to a board committee's charter. It states the purpose of the committee, what the expected results are, what tasks are involved, and the milestones and timelines for success. In addition, it describes who the members should be, not by name but by experience, management level, and other conditions. The charter should express clear accountability to the CEO, board, or executive committee, depending on who can best support the ESOP committee for success.

Along with a charter, there should be a budget for implementing activities to improve organizational effectiveness and communication. When setting up the budget, senior leaders should view these dollars as an investment in future earnings by getting buy-in for change. For example, one company suffering through the recession of 2009–10 needed to cut expenses, including the committee's budget. When senior leaders discussed these proposed cuts with the committee and their constituencies, they agreed that other areas could be cut to keep up morale and increase the levels of support for the cuts that were coming. That is why it is important for ESOP committees to have a senior-level sponsor or member to ensure that well-thought-out activities are funded and executed. When the company has to test its ownership culture, having an effective ESOP committee can actually *save* money in later years.

Developing a Meeting Agenda

Developing a meeting agenda is simple to describe but complex in execution. At the end of the meeting, the next meeting's agenda should be developed so there is accountability for finishing agreed-upon activities before the next meeting. It also saves time later when the leader must produce minutes of the meeting and is chasing down people for input on the next agenda. The agenda checklist below may help you plan your next meeting.

Agenda Checklist

1. Review the agenda and last meeting minutes.
2. Recognize team members present and absent.
3. Review the committee's performance and promises from the last meeting.
4. Review current action items, both ongoing and completed.
5. Continue with problem-solving, brainstorming, or other activities based on their timelines.
6. Identify outstanding items for the next meeting and any new items to add for the next meeting.
7. Create an agenda for the next meeting.

Managing the Meeting

The role of the committee chair is to encourage discussion and prevent dominant members from overwhelming the group. Committee chairs should not allow people to be silent and avoid contributing to the discussion. For a committee to be engaged, members must be free to express their thoughts without fear, and this is a powerful argument that the chair of the committee should not be the CEO or another senior manager. When a senior manager is the chair, his or her ability to help get buy-in from members will be reduced because people will not participate actively if they fear being punished or even terminated if they speak up.

Thus, although a senior manager may sometimes at least temporarily be a good fit on the committee, usually it is more effective to allow a more junior person be the chair, to help develop his or her leadership skills for personal development and to provide a teaching opportunity for the senior manager to help a future leader. The most effective ESOP companies use the ESOP committee membership as a career development and leadership opportunity to help educate and communicate more effectively.

The committee chair should not be in charge of taking notes for the committee's minutes. Once the committee approves the minutes, they should be posted in a prominent location, such as the punch clock area or cafeteria, so employees see the committee is performing. Below are suggested agenda items for the leader to review to ensure a successful meeting:

- What needs to be finished at this meeting?
- Is the location and time set?
- For long meetings, have the breaks been added?
- Is the agenda sent out before the meeting?
- Are the activities well defined and agenda topics prioritized?
- Will you allow new items on the agenda?
- How will you ensure participation?
- Are the refreshments arranged for a long meeting?

- Does each member know what to bring?
- Do you have enough people to have a meeting?
- Is the person who will write up the minutes going to be there?
- What information are you missing?
- Are all of the presentation equipment and tools available and ready?

Suggested Rules for Committee Members

One of the early activities of the committee when it is forming or adding new members is to go over the rules for being an ESOP committee member. My suggested rules are:

- All members must receive and have read the ESOP's summary plan description.
- During meetings, the leader will ensure one person speaks at a time, without interruption.
- Members are expected to listen well and ask questions when appropriate.
- The leader must ensure the meetings start on time and end on time.
- Members and the leader will stick to the topic at hand and remind each other when this rule is being broken.
- Everyone has the responsibility to contribute; the leader should not have to prompt you to get involved.
- The committee leader's responsibility is to encourage participation, not dominate the discussions or direction of activities.
- Each member must commit to speaking clearly, with candor, without malice or value judgments.
- If you need to run the meetings via a conference call process, give only two minutes for other members to call in, and then make the roll call. People coming in late need to be advised that their tardiness caused the group harm because their contributions and understanding were not available.

- Some of the best technologies for having great meetings to-day involve teleconferencing applications using webcams and Internet-based video services such as Google Voice and Skype. If your company has multiple locations, it should investigate having meetings in this manner if it is not already doing so. It saves on time, travel expenses, and other costs. Create rules to work under these conditions. For example, one company speci-fied that people who work out of their homes dress up for the video meeting and not wear pajamas.

- New members should go through an orientation process to help advance their institutional knowledge as quickly as possible. This process should include introductions and meetings with the CEO, the trustee(s), and the committee chair.

- The process should include a committee book, a collection of information such as the summary plan description, the commit-tee's charter, past minutes of the meeting, and other historical stories or activities for people to learn from.

- All members must bring a smile and a funny story that can be shared before the meeting starts, especially when times are tough, the company is struggling with difficult conditions, and the need for change and reduction of expenses dominates people's spirit and emotions.

- Using staggered terms for committee membership will allow in-stitutional knowledge to continue while the membership chang-es. Term limits from one to five years are common, depending on the company's culture and how senior management wants to embrace an empowered or engaged committee. I suggest using three-year terms, with a limit of two consecutive terms, so that over five years, the committee adjusts to the organizational change and becomes accountable to its evolving leadership style.

- The committee's composition should include those employee-owners who seek to improve the ESOP's ownership culture through their participation. By having a cross-functional mem-bership where all divisions, departments, and management levels are reflected, the committee can execute activities and changes with fewer mistakes and less resistance.

- Make sure a vice chair is identified to help stabilize leadership transitions, which may be planned or may surface abruptly. Grooming the future leader is the most important activity of a current committee leader. To develop into a future leader, an identified successor must observe and then gradually experience key leadership activities so he or she provides a smooth transition, without disruption or surprises, when assuming the position of chair.

Dealing with Specific Issues

The following section discusses various challenges and issues that arise and how to approach them, sometimes illustrated with a real-life example from an ESOP company. Keep in mind, however, that as noted above, what works in one company may not work in another.

Tough Times

One ESOP company found that the volume of customer orders was collapsing as the economy collapsed. The company was slashing budgets, and the CEO was advised to ask for suggestions from the company's teams and ESOP committee, which were functioning well. From their recommendations, the company was able to keep its workforce reduction to less than 10% of staff, and it found more savings than it had targeted. By having the goodwill and communication systems in place, the ESOP committee was able to share its story well and get buy-in for rapid change. By not laying off more people, the company was able to retain the expertise to meet customer demand when it returned 15 months later.

Levels of Ownership

At another company, the ESOP owned less than 30%, and yet the company had an engaged ESOP committee that won ESOP awards for best practices in communicating the ESOP. The original owner's predisposition for having the ESOP made it easier for the committee to embrace an ownership culture and enjoy the fruits of its effort.

In contrast, another company was about 30% owned by its ESOP, but its original owners were not interested in engaging in an ownership culture and populated the ESOP committee with key executives. Their top-down approach still produced profits and sales growth, and their value was understood by management and staff. This professional firm, consisting mostly of engineers, had employee engagement, but due to the nature of its industry and employee membership, it was less focused on communicating the ESOP than it was on building revenues and share value. It did not have conflicts in the organization because it had a cohesive group of engaged leaders who did not need a highly functional ESOP committee.

Some 100% ESOP-owned companies use their ESOP committees to improve employee morale through innovative communication techniques. In other 100% ESOP-owned companies, the ESOP committee is still run by the same leadership as before the ESOP owned a majority of shares.

In some cases, the founder is not willing to engage the ESOP committee because the ESOP was primarily a financial tool serving an estate plan, and sharing the wealth was a lower priority. The ESOP committee did not engage well with the organization, and yet the stock price kept growing.

In short, what works in one company may not work well for others. Challenges of leadership can be found in any organization, including those with ESOPs. Only over time will change occur. Many will want immediate change, but only the power of the leader drives what kind of culture he or she wants to achieve. Enlightened, trustworthy, and self-confident leaders, rather than those with command-and-control management styles, are more likely to have an engaged ESOP committee and higher morale among employees.

Different Employee Groups

Many companies have an inadvertent separation of employee classes based on age, longevity, or union membership (union issues are discussed below). This separation of groups can create struggles in an ESOP committee. The committee desires to create an ownership culture that embraces empowerment and contribution, while the separation creates resistance, conflict, and/or organizational dysfunction. The situation is similar to that of the in-laws or adopted children of a wealthy family. The employees who feel separate can have negative emotions caused by mistreatment, lack of respect, or other behaviors that promote one group over another. Having token members of the "out" group on the committee can backfire if those people go back to their group and express mistreatment and isolation. One way to improve their condition is to select the person in that group with the most respect, power, and influence (not necessarily authority), so he or she, if heard, listened to, and allowed to contribute to new ideas, will engage the "out" group in ways authority figures could not.

Management and Ownership Transitions

During the transitions of ownership and management, organizational tension rises. People wonder who will take over, what will happen to the company, and what will happen to them. The ESOP committee can be instrumental in smoothing out concerns over change, job security, and the future of the company. Managers are in charge of managing complexity and systems, whereas leaders have a vision and attract people to that vision. When a company has an owner and/or management change, it is imperative that the ESOP committee helps to promote continuity by providing a clear vision that inspires people to follow. This may require management and the committee to increase their levels of communication and coordinate their messages to ensure consistency. The board should also be active with the committee and engage with the trustee to ensure that accurate and properly developed messages are presented and questions answered with candor.

Family Issues

In some ESOP companies, the ownership and leadership of the company are controlled by the founding family. The family may have used the tax benefits of selling to the ESOP to buy out a family member or to share the wealth with employees who helped build the value the family now enjoys. The ESOP committee may not have the freedom or ability to engage an ownership culture if the controlling family fears loss of control. At one company, the founder promised the presidency to his oldest son in his early years, only to find later that the son was not capable of being the president. The family issues affected the leadership team, with several top managers threatening to leave if the son became president. The ESOP committee had to deal with these and other issues as it attempted to improve communication of the values of being an ESOP. Having attempted to apply best practices, the committee began to get frustrated, with some members not attending committee meetings and even having conflicting meetings outside the building. Only after the issues of leadership and control were clarified and communicated did the ESOP committee revive.

Union Issues

Companies with unions often find there is a moderate level of tension between the ESOP committee and union employees who are not participating in the ESOP. Some companies are nevertheless able to engage with the union membership on ESOP information. Other companies experience high levels of conflict with management, resulting in a lack of trust and contention for change.

In many ways, the committee's hands are tied. An ESOP committee may be constrained by law in the ways that it engages union members. Collective bargaining agreements also may restrict the committee from involving union members regarding retirement benefits. (Chapter 1 of this book covers some of the challenges of the committee when dealing with union.) In my experience, companies with collective bargaining agreements have such different relationships with their rank-and-file members that what may work with one company will not work with others. I suggest that the committee chair and the senior executive who is a sponsor of the committee educate the committee on the correct way of engaging union members.

In one case, an ESOP company had multiple locations with union representation, as well as nonunion locations. The company president was on the ESOP committee decades ago, when the company transitioned to being 100% ESOP-owned. Communication was difficult for the committee. It asked the union representative for permission to speak to the members on their recent change to a 100% ESOP and to offer them participation in the ESOP. The union leadership had no interest and advised the committee to not speak to the union members. This decision led to a separation of the workforce both in benefits and in information sharing. Over time, the committee's efforts to communicate with the nonunion rank and file facilitated the union members' growing interest in learning more. By the time the company decided to upgrade its ownership culture with teams, the relationship with the union was still contentious, but many rank-and-file employees were willing and interested in sitting in classes to learn empowered teamwork. The ESOP committee's patient and careful efforts to communicate with all employees, regardless of membership, resulted in a more positive work environment.

When a company with a collective bargaining agreement implements an ESOP, the committee should do the following:

- Do not have high expectations for trust and agreement with union representatives in the early stages of ESOP transitions. We suggest you keep your efforts consistent and transparent so that over time, union members will gain interest in learning more.

- Focus on the noneconomic benefits of having an ESOP that best fit your organization. Job security and career opportunities are just two of many benefits ESOPs provide.

- When dealing with the union representative or business agent, prepare all discussions in writing in advance. Without such preparation, many times the union staff may not recall or may misunderstand the verbal requests from the committee members, resulting in high levels of confusion and frustration. For example, in one instance, the union denied management ever offered to invite the union members to learn about the ESOP and its benefits.

- Make sure each presentation in subsequent offers for participation to union members and their representatives is in writing, in advance of discussions, and be clear as to the purpose of the offer or request. In some cases, union leaders may have communicated a difference of opinion with the company, so having it in writing helps clarify the committee's intent and information. Above all, be honest and transparent with your needs and desired results.

What Information to Share

Determining how much information to shares is a common issue with every company, whether an ESOP or not. One can compare it with owning a car. If you are the owner, can you answer the following questions: What year is the car? What kind of gas does the manufacturer recommend? What is the mileage? When was the last oil change? How many spark plugs does it have? What are the tire sizes? What is the proper air pressure for the tires? Does it have air conditioning? How about power windows and locks? Depending on your level of sophistication and knowledge, you may answer all the questions quickly and correctly, or you may not answer correctly or not have answers for others. It is important to know what is important to be an owner. Someone who fixes his or her own cars can answer all these questions correctly. Others, who pay a mechanic, may answer a few questions and ignore the importance of other questions. The same can be said with financials and other proprietary company information.

Whatever you share with employee-owners will unquestionably be available for your competition. With today's technologies, private information is readily shared on Web sites, including your own. For example, many companies put their newsletters on their Web sites.

At a minimum, the ESOP committee should share the value of the stock in the plan, and each individual's value, shares, and vested amount in a statement on a one-on-one basis, not in the newsletter. Having a quarterly "town hall meeting" including presentations by members of the committee will help as well. Committees should also share the summary plan description and have a shareholder's meeting to publicly explain where the company has been over the past year. You may also share who the new employees are and any management promotions as part of the information.

If you have a more engaged and open team environment, then you may want to add more detailed financial information as well as projected opportunities. However, companies should not share too much, as it may give the company's competition an opportunity to undermine the company itself. Including the company's change efforts, like team-building or Six Sigma, in a newsletter is a great way to share stories. On the other hand, identifying new products or services in a newsletter can be harmful if the competition reads about it. Sharing customer names, financial information, or new locations may harm the company by providing competitors an advantage. Newsletters are a great way of sharing information; however, if a competitor reads and learns company secrets after reading a newsletter, is it worth it? Again, the management style (command and control versus an empowered management team) will drive the answers to these questions and concerns. Chapter 4 of this book covers these issues well. Open-book management activities are great for the right organization. Open-book management is best taught only when a company's managers are ready to engage their employee-owners to rise to the next level.

Conflicts of Interest

Occasionally, an ESOP committee member may have an agenda that benefits him or her personally over the interests of the committee. Serving on an ESOP committee is often an honor to its members, and many seek to foster collegiality and a spirit of teamwork. In this atmosphere, challenging a dominating member with or without authority can be very difficult and uncomfortable. A conflict of interest arises when an individual or organization has multiple interests, the advancement of one of which could be at the expense of the other. One way to test the objectivity of an idea or suggestion is to determine whether it meets the Rotary Club's "Four-Way Test."

Boards and committees should follow this test to improve trust in the committee:

1. Is it the *truth?*
2. Is it *fair* to all concerned?
3. Will it build *goodwill* and *better friendships?*
4. Will it be *beneficial* to all concerned?

If you are a member of the committee and are troubled by the actions, behaviors, or suggestions of one or more members, this popular tool can help explore the issues that are troubling you in a nonthreatening way. Great leaders can sense conflicts and adjust their approaches once they realize the difficulty their agendas or recommendations are creating.

CHAPTER 6

ESOP Committees: Stages of Development

Stephen Clifford, Christopher Mackin, and Camille Kerr

As previous chapters demonstrate, there are many factors to consider in building an ESOP committee that is effective and well suited to your company. The type of the committee, mission and vision statements, leadership structure, and company culture all play a part in how successful the committee will be. Many of these factors are decided when the committee is founded and will remain the same over the life of the committee. However, a committee's success is not solely determined by early decisions.

Committees change over time. Strategies that were successful early on may not yield the same results as the committee matures. An ESOP committee must be dynamic and adaptive to remain effective. This chapter discusses the common challenges that committees face as they progress, and best practices for dealing with those challenges.

While each committee will develop in its own way according to the interests of the members and the formal responsibility and authority delegated to it, like most groups, ESOP committees follow a pattern of development. The pattern mirrors the stages of human development, including infancy,[1] adolescence, adulthood, and then older adulthood.[2] Each of these phases carries its own unique challenges.

---

1. The reference to "infancy" is not a statement about the maturity of the group members, but the development of the group as a whole.

2. Richard C. Weber, "The Group: A Cycle from Birth to Death," in *Reading Book for Human Relations Training* (Arlington, VA: National Training Laboratories, 1982), 68–71.

The goal of this chapter is to help your company diagnose what stage your committee is in, avoid common pitfalls associated with that stage, and give your company the tools it needs to address issues that are likely to arise in the future. ESOP committees that properly apply these principles can consistently encourage employee involvement, increase understanding of employees' attitudes toward ownership, contribute to a healthy ownership culture, and build and maintain a high-performance work environment.

Overview of the Development Process

An ESOP committee's development will depend greatly on its structure, mission, leadership, and company culture. But regardless of its particular characteristics, the committee will likely experience a predictable pattern of development. Like an individual, an ESOP committee goes through infancy, adolescence, adulthood, and older adulthood.[3]

In the infancy stage, members of the recently established committee are developing their positions and respective roles, and forming their identities within the committee. The majority of the committee's actions at this stage are in response to external demands, not guided by the committee itself. It is a somewhat productive, cautious stage. As the group develops its own independence and identity, it transitions into the adolescent stage, which brings heightened energy and an abundance of new ideas but may also bring about interpersonal difficulties. The committee will explore its boundaries and the range of possibilities for its future, but it may be only moderately productive regarding its goals and mission.

As the committee matures, it will grow comfortable with its limitations and focus more clearly on a few realistic objectives. As the interpersonal issues resolve, the group will enter its most pro-

---

3.   The stages also share common ground with B.W. Tuckman's familiar "forming, storming, norming, performing" format, where forming corresponds with infancy, storming with adolescence, norming with a transitional period between adolescence and adulthood, and performing with adulthood. See B.W. Tuckman, "Development Sequence in Small Groups," *Psychological Bulletin* 63 (1965): 284–399.

ductive stage, adulthood.[4] Stage 3 is the longest stage of the group's development. However, it is not permanent. Over time, many committees lose their earlier energy and creativity, and move into the fourth stage, older adulthood, where there is resistance to change, a loss of appetite for new challenges, and possibly a regression to earlier stages.[5]

While this framework helps illustrate the typical growth pattern of a committee, none of the stages has a clear line separating it from the others, and there is no typical timeline for moving through the stages. Committees will progress at vastly different paces. Furthermore, progress through the stages is not likely to be linear and direct. Most ESOP committees take a few steps forward then at least one back. Often, the regression and repeating of an earlier stage will help build trust and confidence, leading to greater cohesion and trust among members, and as a result, greater productivity.

How the Type of Committee Affects the Development Process

One of the most influential early decisions is whether the committee will primarily serve an administrative function, a communications function, or a combination of the two. The two types of committees are described in depth in part 1 of this book. For purposes of this

---

4.   In between adolescence and adulthood is the "norming" stage in the Tuckman model. Since it is a transitional phase, we have not chosen to give it its own stage in this model. In the human development analogy, the "norming" stage is the time during which the individual is becoming an adult and at different times behaves "adult-like" and at others "adolescent-like."

5.   A succinct summary of the Tuckman model of group development appeared in an issue of *Training and Development:* "In the forming stage, new groups may have high morale even before they start to address the task at hand. In the storming stage, there may be competition for roles and there may be recognition of performance shortcomings that cause discomfort among team members. In the norming stage, teams establish some roles and procedural standards as they begin to accomplish their tasks. In the final stage, performing, both morale and competence are high as teams begin to achieve the performance levels expected." Harlan R. Jessup, "The Road to Results for Teams," *Training and Development* 46, no. 9 (September 1992): 65.

section, we will provide a brief description of each type of committee and how the type of committee affects the development process.

ESOP administrative committees often, but not necessarily, have a legal responsibility to run the ESOP and are considered fiduciaries. This responsibility often forces rapid initial growth and clarifies the group's responsibilities. Often, these committees demonstrate considerably fewer of the symptoms of committee development. However, each group is likely to experience some of the common stages.

With administrative committees, formal or informal training is often a fundamental part of the committee's early activities. During this training, which often occurs during the process of establishing the ESOP, the committee members learn about the laws that allow for the creation of the ESOP. The committee becomes familiar with the legal limitations of its control and decision-making discretion. When the ESOP administrative committee has not been involved in establishing the ESOP, formal training is especially important to ensure the committee members fully understand the implications of their actions.

Because of the early training and defined scope of their decision-making responsibilities, administrative committees often experience the stages of committee development in more subtle ways. Additionally, the formal need to make decisions about ESOP design forces the group into a highly productive stage very early on.

Communications committees, on the other hand, experience a more typical development. Again, part 1 of this book includes an in-depth discussion of the role of a communications committee, but briefly, a cultural change-oriented committee is generally responsible for encouraging and fostering a strong sense of ownership among company employees and assisting in building increased productivity and profitability. Some ESOP communications committees are responsible only for planning events, notices, newsletters, and other forms of communication. Others facilitate employee input, advise management, and may serve a governance role. Either way, these types of committees can make a significant contribution to building an ownership culture and adding to company success. A good ESOP communications committee can expand communication throughout the organization.

A Few Tips to Keep in Mind

Before delving into the stages, it is helpful to consider the following tips, which are applicable throughout the lifetime of a committee.

- *Sustain energy.* The most important thing to keep in mind throughout the process is to sustain energy. Energy can be expressed in positive and negative ways. Often in stages 1 and 2, this energy is expressed negatively, as conflict or frustration. While the tensions can be difficult to deal with, they express a level of enthusiasm that needs to be embraced. If negative energy is suppressed, it can turn to apathy, which is the downfall of many committees. It is important to encourage the commitment while trying to refocus it in more positive directions.

- *Let it grow.* The second tip to keep in mind is that the committee must develop its own identity, informal rules, decision-making process, and confidence. While it is important for stakeholders and company leaders to support the committee and demonstrate a genuine interest in it, those who are not a part of the committee must let it grow and take responsibility for its own projects. Excessive intervention is a common pitfall throughout the stages. While well intentioned, such intervention can prevent the committee from developing a sense of responsibility for the projects and ideas it pursues. The result is excessive dependency on outsiders, which will hinder the committee's ability to form properly and will keep it in the early stages of development, making any real accomplishments unlikely. In the words of one practitioner, "Unwittingly, you can become the group's internal expert, coach, change agent, manager of internal difficulties and so forth. The more you respond in those ways, the more the group will look to you to handle those tasks. The more you take on, the less likely that the team will gain the skills it needs."[6]

- *Keep it focused.* ESOP committee discussions can grow in a wide range of directions. Many of these discussions can be highly

---

6. Rosaria Taraschi, "Cutting the Ties That Bind," *Training and Development* 52, no. 11 (November 1998): 12.

productive, especially in the earlier stages of development. However, to avoid wasting time on irrelevant issues, it is often useful to keep the overall goals and mission of the committee in the forefront of each member's mind. While the facilitator or leader is ultimately responsible for this, one simple, effective approach is to place it at the top or bottom of every printed agenda or meeting notes page. This is especially effective if the ESOP committee keeps careful notes. It is another opportunity to subtly remind members and the entire company of the overall mission of the group and to keep the group focused on that mission.

With that as background, we now turn to a detailed description of the various stages of committee development.

The Development Process

Stage 1: Infancy

The initial stage of group development is infancy. It is a stage of timidity and identity development. As previously mentioned, the committee is unlikely to initiate action on its own at this stage. It will primarily rely on outsiders to recommend action. Also, committee members may be more concerned about their personal reasons for membership on the committee and why the committee exists than they are with achieving the goals of the committee.[7]

ESOP committees are often created when managers recognize that they alone cannot fully meet the challenge of building an effective ownership culture. To enjoy the benefits of effective employee ownership, the company—and its management team—needs to better understand the workforce and its perceived relationship with the company. Thus a committee is formed to help management better understand how employees feel about the company and ownership.

Often, the first responsibility of the committee is to help plan an announcement or training program that will introduce employees to the ESOP. The company leaders requesting the program and seeking to make it as effective as possible are essentially running

---

7. Jessup, "The Road to Results for Teams," 65.

the committee at this stage. Committee members, unsure of their responsibilities and influence, tentatively respond to questions and keep many of their personal opinions to themselves.

In this stage, the committee will inevitably struggle with its specific mission and with the extent to which it is responsible to be an activist organization advocating employee concerns and interests to management. These issues may be exacerbated in committees where members were appointed or selected by management. They may fear that they will be removed from it if they express strong opinions that conflict with the manager(s) who created the committee and selected them to serve on it. Thus, while group members may respond to the questions about the program presented, their primary concern is: "How am I supposed to act and react without jeopardizing my personal position?"

Further, in the infancy stage, group members are learning to relate to one another in a new context. For many nonmanagerial employees, the committee environment is new and uncomfortable. While many of the committee members may be acquainted with each other, they do not know what to expect from each other in this new context. This is where the group members discover their common purpose and concerns. Members begin to identify themselves as a group and start to work out an internal structure and subgroup identities as members find allies with common concerns and interests.

Pitfalls

Excessive intervention. In the infancy stage, it is likely that productivity as measured by the committee's mission and goals will be low. Often, in order to encourage a common sense of accomplishment, the manager or group that created the committee will make recommendations and suggestions. These suggestions often lead to short-term achievements, which can build a sense of pride and accomplishment in the group. However, while the motivation is good, and the results may be positive in the short term, such recommendations and suggestions can be counterproductive with regard to the team.

The ESOP committee needs to develop through the infancy stage on its own. Intervention from outsiders can shortchange the development process, and contribute to a sense of dependence in the group.[8] In the long term, dependence on an outsider is likely to dampen committee motivation and limit the sense of individual responsibility for the committee's success. Such dependency undermines the group process and prevents the committee from getting started.

The group needs to work out its own relationships. A good facilitator must maintain group rules, let the group members work out interpersonal issues, and provide an atmosphere where they can find their new roles within the group.

Unclear goals. In the infancy stage, committee members seek common goals to understand why they are together. When the goals and mission of the group are unclear, the committee is likely to flounder. It is often helpful for the creator of the ESOP committee to clarify the mission of the committee and how it fits into the company's long-term goals. Once the mission is clear, the group can begin to plan its actions in line with that mission. In the process, the group will rally around the common goals and have productive discussions while they work out their interpersonal issues and roles.

Often, it is extremely productive for a committee in its beginning stages to clarify concrete short-term goals based on the overall mission.[9] Such goals can be a highly productive way to encourage the group to come together, accelerate the process of development through this initial stage, and help establish a framework for future work together. Jon Katzenback explains the power of this function clearly: "Transforming broad directives into specific and measurable performance goals is the surest first step for a team trying to shape a purpose meaningful to its members."[10]

Unclear membership selection process. The infancy stage is when ESOP committee members struggle to define the group and themselves

---

8.   Taraschi, "Cutting the Ties That Bind," 12.

9.   J.R. Katzenbach and D.K. Smith, "The Discipline of Teams," *Harvard Business Review* 71, no. 2 (March-April 1993): 111.

10.   Ibid.

within it. Insecurity abounds when the committee members do not understand how or why they were selected for it. It is exacerbated when it is unclear how or why they can be removed or replaced. ESOP committee membership is often perceived as a privilege and implies authority and trust. Nobody wants to have that privilege revoked, but without a transparent selection process, members are likely to feel insecure and fail to invest their full energy and commitment into the committee.

Unclear rules. Since infancy is the first step, and the members are defining themselves within the group, it is critical that the ground rules be clear and carefully maintained (preferably by a competent facilitator). Unclear ground rules will undermine trust and impede the committee's effectiveness. Some members will likely not participate fully in the process because they do not feel personally responsible for the outcome.

Suggestions

Train the committee. Often, the difficulties that accompany the infancy phase can be mitigated with well-planned group activities, training, and meetings. These meetings need to include an opportunity for members to get to know each other informally, as well as an informational component that addresses how they are expected to work together. Familiarity among members is extremely useful in fostering rapid growth of cooperative attitudes and efforts.[11] Often ESOP committee training provides the opportunity to "break the ice" and allows members to learn about each other in a new context. Further, it is an opportunity to give the group some of the tools that will help it in future stages. Examples of effective training include effective communication methods; ground rules for committee meetings; problem solving and decision making processes; and tools to generate and evaluate ideas, seek the root causes of problems,

---

11. R.A. Guzzo and M.W. Dickson, "Teams in Organizations Recent Research on Performance and Effectiveness," *Annual Review of Psychology* 47 (Annual 1996): 307.

and generate possible solutions. Some very successful committees have spent months or even years training before starting a project.

Start with an exciting, simple project. Early successes bring the committee members together. Suggesting the committee begin with a straightforward educational or celebratory event (but allowing the committee to accomplish the project itself) will bring about greater enthusiasm about the committee and its mission.

Stage 2: Adolescence

In the adolescent phase, ESOP committee members have developed a sense of the committee's purpose and have begun to unify around some common goals. However, despite this progress, the adolescent phase is often the most difficult and uncomfortable stage in committee development because of interpersonal differences about the direction of the committee and the respective roles committee members will have moving forward. Individual committee members may want to have more influence over how decisions are made, or they may want to change the committee's general direction. In the process, internal alliances can develop, and these alliances may clash on a number of issues. While this stage is often uncomfortable and difficult, it is critical to development of an effective team; members learn important lessons for future decision-making.

The difficulties often revolve around which committee goals to pursue first. In the infancy phase, the committee has likely developed a series of goals that all agree are important. However, individuals and sub-groups will disagree over which goals are most important. The conflicts that emerge from these differences are valuable to the committee's development. It may be uncomfortable, and appear unproductive, but managing these early conflicts is instructional for the future.

Pitfalls

Excessive intervention. When serious conflicts emerge, stakeholders and company leaders often want to get involved. Although it is tempting, intervening will prevent the group from working through this difficult stage and create a pattern of dependence. The committee will start to rely on the ability to call in an external authority figure to mediate conflicts. This dependence will inhibit group development and undermine the committee members' sense of personal responsibility for the group.[12]

Unclear rules. The committee's rules and boundaries become even more important in the adolescent stage of development. Just as adolescents push the boundaries of their parents' authority, the committee members and the committee itself will start to challenge the rules. At this point, the internal ground rules need to be clear, and the committee's authority (and its limits) must also be carefully defined and maintained.

Unknown process. Many groups struggle in the adolescent phase to work out how they will make decisions and move forward. Often these struggles can be eased if the committee understands and accepts a common decision-making process. For example: Will the group make decisions based on a majority vote or is broader consensus required? The procedures should not just be limited to the vote, however. Members should receive training on how to define objectives, generate ideas, discuss alternatives, and reach a common decision. The content of the decision-making process is less important than ensuring that all members accept it.

Splinters and schisms. Sometimes during the adolescent phase, members withdraw either because of excessive intervention or serious conflict. When this happens, individuals and sub-groups may refuse to productively participate in the committee. It is important in these situations to restore the withdrawn members to the committee. Unless the individual is brought back, it is unlikely that the committee will move beyond the adolescent stage. Also, when certain members are driven out, splinter groups and schisms may appear. These groups are extremely capable of undermining the committee's effectiveness. The individuals chosen for the ESOP committee carry

---

12. Taraschi, "Cutting the Ties That Bind," 12.

credibility and informal (or formal) authority with their peers. If they are not fully on board or are actively undermining the efforts of the committee, at least partial failure is inevitable.

Suggestions

Bear with it! As with human development, the adolescent phase is often the most difficult for ESOP committees. It is critical to keep everyone involved and active without preventing or avoiding disagreements that are important to the committee's development.

Accept moderate levels of conflict. In addition to understanding that conflict is necessary in this phase, the facilitator needs to be aware that the capacity for conflict will differ in each group member. Therefore, without dampening the disagreement, it is important to keep conflict to a level at which everyone (or nearly everyone) feels only a little uncomfortable. Keeping the conflict at a manageable level will prevent the schisms discussed above. While group members can be brought back in if they withdraw at this point, it will result in regression, and possibly having to go through the adolescent stage again. Training in the principles of committee development can help committee members understand what is happening and realize that the conflict is necessary and natural—not a sign that the group is a failure.

Stage 3: Adulthood

Stage 3 is the adult phase. While the transition from infancy to adolescence is clearly marked by conflict, the development into adulthood is less clearly defined. Just as older adolescents will sometimes act as adults and other times act as adolescents, so too will the committee.[13] Adulthood begins as the group grows more comfortable with its new self-imposed rules and gets down to real work on the mission

---

13. Tuckman includes a stage between stage 2 and stage 3 called "norming." The norming stage is when team members grow comfortable with their common rules and boundaries. The power struggles are largely worked through and the members, now comfortable in their roles within the committee, begin to settle into the real work at hand.

and goals. Interpersonal issues are (mostly) worked out—committee members have learned how to work together and disagree without causing division or emotional injury.

The adult phase of committee development is where the most productive work will get done. The committee members now initiate their own ideas, activities, and projects, in contrast to the infancy phase, where the committee relied on external motivations. Additionally, the committee's focus is on the mission and goals of the committee and the company overall, as opposed to personal motivations or insecurities. The group has clarified its own informal rules (within the formal boundaries originally established), and members have internalized them. The committee has also defined its decision-making process (around the framework originally presented in training) and participants have accepted it.

As the group moves more securely into adulthood, its productivity and success will lead to increased enthusiasm and pride. Members will feel more responsible for the work of the committee and for the success of the decisions and programs it implements. Committee members will exhibit high levels of mutual trust and respect for one another, truly embrace the goals, and pursue them with energy and vigor. High levels of trust are most evident when the group is brainstorming new ideas—the brainstorming is fast and furious, and ideas are blurted out, recorded, and built upon, leading to impressive creativity and energy.

Unfortunately, it is impossible for the committee to arrive here unless it has first experienced the other stages of development, and ESOP committees are likely to regress partially to the adolescent stage from time to time. When a new member joins, the committee may regress to adolescence or even infancy if the reason for the new member's inclusion is not clear. Furthermore, regression to infancy is almost inevitable if a committee member is removed or replaced, unless the reasons for this removal are transparent, credible, and well understood by the group as a whole.

Experiencing regression may seem frustrating, but is actually a good sign. Each time the group goes through the adolescent phase, the trust and confidence of the members will grow. In fact, some of the most productive ESOP committees demonstrate constant, fluid shifts between adolescence and adulthood. With each shift, group cohesion grows and the discomfort of adolescence seems to inspire greater energy and creativity.

Pitfalls

Forcing the group into adulthood. Clearly, adulthood is the ideal phase, and every committee hopes to stay there permanently. It is where the committee achieves success and a genuine esprit de corps. However, it is nearly inevitable that the group will move tentatively back and forth into the adult stage and back to the adolescent stage. In time, it will grow to spend more time in the adult stage, until most of its time is spent there. The group must arrive at the adult stage on its own, and forced progress into the adult stage is likely to splinter the group, lead to dependence on the facilitator or leader,[14] or cause a number of members to withdraw.

Changes in the committee members. Committee members are likely to change over time. Some members' professional responsibilities will change, making it impossible for them to continue, and making the inclusion of others valuable. Each new member creates a new group, and the group will likely at least partially regress to adolescence until the new members' position in the group is clarified formally and informally. Often, a number of personnel changes occur simultaneously. These major changes take the group back a stage or two. Unless the group is allowed the time to process these changes, it will feel forced into adulthood, leading to the problems mentioned above.

Lack of support and resources. Committee resources include the amount of time that personnel such as management, chairpersons, and/or facilitators can provide; the amount of hours members may spend on committee work (inside and outside of meetings); and financial resources. When the ESOP committee reaches adulthood, its needs for external support and resources are likely to increase. Members will call for additional information and time to work on

---

14. Rosaria Taraschi, "Cutting the Ties That Bind," p. 12.

new projects. The company should anticipate allotting additional assistance, resources, and time to work on committee projects. If these resources are not forthcoming, the members will become frustrated and lose energy.

Suggestions

Maintain appropriate boundaries. In the adult phase, the committee's needs may go beyond the resources that can be allocated to it. Therefore, it is important to maintain appropriate boundaries for the resources it can use. To reduce the frustration at this stage, it is helpful to explain the extent of available resources in the early stages or the initial training. If these boundaries are clear at the outset, the committee's expectations will be realistic, and its energy will be focused on projects within its resources. On the other hand, if new boundaries on resources are imposed at this stage, they may appear arbitrary to the committee members, and leave them frustrated, disappointed, and disillusioned with the process. As a result, the group will probably slide back a stage or two since members will question the purpose of the committee and their role in it.

Allow failure. It is important to support committee initiatives with the resources available, even if they seem flawed. When committee projects receive selective support from the management team, there is often frustration, disappointment, and disillusionment, causing regression. Finally, failure is a good learning experience for the committee. Its members will learn (as most people do) more lessons from failure than from success.

Share past experiences. Often, the ESOP committee will come up with ideas that have been tried before. When this happens, give the committee a chance to learn from the past experiences. Simply giving a manager time to talk with the committee can help the group identify possible problems in its plan and deal with unforeseen difficulties. The goal is to provide the committee with all of the resources possible to succeed, including management experience and expertise. The phrase "that didn't work last time we tried it" is of little value.

In addition, many projects that have been unsuccessful in the past as management initiatives may be more successful if the ESOP committee designs and implements them.

Make use of subcommittees and task forces. Often subcommittees and task forces can be helpful in the adult phase. After a project has been identified, a subgroup of the committee (which can also include noncommittee members) can be created to implement the project. While subcommittees can cause schisms during the infancy or adolescent phases, they can be highly productive in this stage. The subcommittee or task force should have a clear goal, a recommended process for attaining that goal, and a specific timeline or "life expectancy" so that once the goal is attained, the subcommittee or task force ceases to exist. The limited lifespan will create a sense of urgency to accomplish its goal within the time constraints imposed upon it by the overall committee and will encourage the subgroup through the stages of development quickly.

Some examples of such subcommittees are "ESOP Month" celebration committees, "ESOP newsletter design" committees, and event planning committees. Subcommittees and task forces can also be created to research and report back to the overall committee. An example of such a committee is one responsible to explore and report on the publications and training programs available to ESOP companies, or the cost of printing new company "employee ownership" T-shirts. It is important that these types of committees have strong credibility with the rest of the overall ESOP committee if their report and recommendations are to have influence. Often, members of subcommittees will have specific technical expertise that is helpful for the individual project but not necessary in the ESOP committee overall.

Stage 4: Older Adulthood

Many ESOP committees enter older adulthood after they have tried some ideas and found limited success. As a result, the committee falters and loses its focus. The lack of success can be due to a failure of the committee to plan, lack of support from management, or unrealistic expectations. Regardless of the cause, older adulthood is very common.

In some ways, this stage looks similar to infancy. Members wonder why they are there and question the purpose of the committee. The committee is likely to become a rubber stamp for management ideas (as it was in the infancy phase), making only nominal suggestions and changes to management initiatives. Once again, members begin to focus on their personal motivations instead of committee goals, while the instigation for new ideas and projects falls on external parties.

Pitfalls

Changing committee membership. Often, the first reaction is to change the committee by bringing in new members. Rapid changes in membership can be destructive to the cohesion developed through the previous stages of development. The fresh ideas may be productive and helpful, but it also may send a message to the remaining committee members that they have failed. Such a message is very likely to cause regression to the adolescent or infant stage, but without the hope for future productivity. What the committee really needs at this point is an opportunity for success—even if it is a small, incremental success.

Assigning projects. Another common reaction is to attempt to jumpstart the committee by assigning it a project to work on. While this approach can successfully focus the committee on a new project, it can also drain it of its independence and energy. Whether the idea will refocus energy or drain it depends on the extent to which the idea is suggested or imposed. To be successful, the committee must feel responsible for the selection of the idea and its implementation. If someone outside the committee proposes a project, the committee may not feel responsible for the project or its success. The committee must embrace the idea, design its implementation, and run it on its own. This way, the committee will feel responsible for the project and its success.

Suggestions

Make sure that the goals are realistic. Encourage the ESOP committee to break down major projects into smaller steps. The importance of clearly defined, realistic, achievable goals is paramount to avoid rapid development into the older adult stage. These individual steps are an opportunity to declare victory, however small.

Celebrate success. Success breeds energy and enthusiasm. ESOP committee successes, even small ones, need to be celebrated. Another means to define incremental successes is regular employee attitude surveys. Such surveys can be simple or complex, internal or administered by outsiders, but the changing results over time will provide the committee an opportunity to declare minor victories, receive formal input on issues that deserve more time and energy, and will help generate new ideas for projects to pursue.

Encourage careful evaluation of projects implemented. Celebrate success and dissect failures. Failure is instructive if the committee identifies the causes of failure. When specific causes of failure are identified, the experience becomes productive and potentially positive rather than simply a disappointment that will drain enthusiasm and energy.

Encourage the committee to find the right project. A committee in older adulthood can be reinvigorated by one successful project. This may be either a new idea or one that surfaced in the past but has been forgotten. It is valuable to keep careful notes of ideas and projects as they progress and as they are prioritized. A project or program once abandoned for lack of resources can often provide the group with a new idea to pursue. Thanks to the insight and lessons learned, the committee can pursue this project with more knowledge, experience, and often with new enthusiasm.

Provide more information. The lack of energy and focus in older adulthood can often be overcome with new and important information. The information provided will likely challenge the committee to find new solutions, ideas, and projects to meet the concerns exhibited in the survey results. Other helpful information includes financial information about the company, the marketplace in which the company operates, or statistics about employee injury, turnover, and absenteeism rates. Each of these topics can reinvigorate new ideas in the committee about how to improve morale.

Conclusion

As each committee develops in its own way, through some rather predictable stages, it can grow into a highly productive force for organizational change. By understanding the phase the ESOP committee is going through, management can lend a more timely and useful hand in helping the committee achieve progress and productivity. For committee members, an understanding of this developmental model can create a context to help understand current dilemmas. Awareness of these stages can reduce a sense of isolation and offer a preview of a future that should be more productive than the challenges of the present.

Research has shown, and anecdotal experience confirms, that an ESOP committee can be instrumental in organizational change. A well-formed, diverse committee that includes members from all levels and divisions of an organization can provide invaluable assistance to any effort to embrace and create a culture of ownership at ESOP companies. ESOP companies that have built a culture of ownership have, in nearly every major study, outperformed their competitors who do not pursue such a culture, or lack meaningful employee ownership.

CHAPTER 7

The Top Nine Mistakes ESOP Committees Make (and How to Avoid Them)

Kellee Kroll

I hear from many companies that they have an ESOP committee, but it has gone stale and lost its momentum. Company leaders wonder what they can do to get the committee motivated again. In my experience, there are nine common reasons why committees fail. Instead of trying to fix something that has broken, let us look at these common reasons and find out how to avoid them before they occur.

Since I grew up in Wisconsin and do like a good piece of cheese, I'm using a cheese analogy for this "top 9" list. Also, since Wisconsin claims 4 of the top 100 of America's largest majority-owned ESOP companies,[1] I think the analogy fits.

1. Seal of Approval

Like any good product, success often depends on having a seal of approval. With food, including cheeses, that seal might come from the American Culinary Federation, Inc. (ACF). If your committee does not have support from leadership, stop right now and consider where this lack of approval may lead. The committee's efforts can only be as effective as the leadership's willingness to support the committee's activities. Most committees have begun at the request of leadership. However, if you are one of the rare committees that

---

1. "The Employee Ownership 100: America's Largest Majority Employee-Owned Companies," NCEO, last modified May 2011, http://www.nceo.org/main/article.php/id/11/.

was self-started, perhaps by a middle level of management, a lack of top leadership support may become a road block for you.

Focus on displaying leadership skills and achieving results from your communication efforts; this may be all you need to gain support to continue your efforts. This will be especially important when you construct an annual budget to implement activities and hold special events. Also, without leadership support, you may lack the credibility needed to gain the respect of the employees and become a resource they use. Start off strong by ensuring you have a seal of approval from top leadership.

2. All Shapes and Sizes

Needs change. Maybe you need a cheese slice for a sandwich, grated cheese for a taco, or snack-sized cheese cubes to munch on. Cheese comes in all shapes and sizes to serve different purposes. In the same respect, you need to get a mix of employees on your committee to represent your workforce. Look at your areas of business and geographic locations. For example, if you have three members of the committee who are part of sales but no one who is from the shipping area, you have a void to fill.

Ensure different perspectives by balancing your members' age groups, gender, and years of service with the company. For example, a good way to develop materials for new hires is to enlist a committee member who has been with the company for only a couple of years. Some representation changes as your plan matures. If your plan is approaching its first year of diversification, check that you have a committee member who meets the requirements of age 55 with 10 years of plan participation. If you don't have all areas represented initially, figure out how you can fill in the gaps along the way.

3. The Right Ingredients

Did you know that if a piece of cheese doesn't contain a certain amount of an enzyme called rennet, it won't be solid?[2] Without this

2. "Cheese," *Wikipedia,* last modified September 15, 2011, http://en.wikipedia.org/wiki/Cheese.

ingredient, it loses consistency and lacks solidity. Cheese is made by following a specific process; not a process that can be developed in a matter of minutes, but a process that took valuable time to develop and complete. This process is eventually written down as a "recipe" to recall the steps and procedures that create a quality end product.

In a similar way, following a "recipe" ensures the right structure to contribute to a committee's success. To create a solid foundation for the committee, you should take the time to define its role and purpose, create a mission statement, and charter how the committee will be structured. Developing a charter involves a number of details, including determining the size of the committee, mix of representation, officer election, length of member terms, and selection of future members. Some committees skip this step and find themselves stumbling to implement this later. One such ESOP committee lost four members within a few months due to business-related needs. Because they hadn't defined how new members would be appointed, they lost valuable time during their busiest season while they struggled to figure this out.

4. Some Good Cheeses Stink . . . at First

Limburger cheese, while smelling really bad, is considered a specialty item and is actually quite palatable. Not everyone in an ESOP company is thrilled about becoming an employee-owner. While some skeptics stink up the workplace with their chronic complaining and find negativity in almost anything, others simply lack understanding about the ESOP.

Instead of avoiding your skeptics like stinky cheese, recruit them. By recruiting skeptics as members of your committee, you can turn them into believers and send a strong message to the rest of your employees. Seeking their input can help identify misunderstandings and gain new insights about how employees perceive the ESOP. Their viewpoints on communication efforts may challenge you, but this valuable information can help you improve your communication efforts and avoid unsuccessful programs. Hopefully, in the process of participating on the committee, they will learn more about the ESOP and see the excitement shared by other employees.

5. Scientific Analysis

For being such a simple food, cheese is full of science. Making a great cheese involves chemistry, biochemistry, and more. In fact, there are graduate-level courses in cheese science. Scientists perform experiments and analyze the results to measure how well something has worked.

You should be open to experimenting new ideas in your communication strategy, but be sure to analyze the results in a tangible way to know whether you are making a difference. Will it suffice to think you've made a difference, or would you rather have evidence of it? To have evidence, think about what can be measured. If your goal is to improve employee involvement, track attendance at meetings. Document the number of employees who participate in ESOP-related activities. Prior years' numbers can be compared to future years to see if your efforts are paying off. If your goal is to improve employees' understanding of the ESOP, document the number of questions received. Depending on the questions asked, fewer questions may be evidence of greater understanding. Alternatively, an increase in questions may be evidence of greater understanding and interest if employees are asking more clarifying and complex questions about the ESOP. This type of hard evidence can be used to measure the value of the committee. In fact, you should consider sharing these measurable results with company leaders to help continue receiving their support of the committee.

6. Write a Review

Just as there are movie reviews, consumer product reviews, and restaurant reviews, there are also cheese reviews. A review lets you know how delicious a kind of cheese is, what flavors it has, and which cheesemaker produces the best of its kind. I encourage you to write your own review each year of the committee's activities. It is crucial that you document the accomplishments and projects completed by your committee to know and remember what produced a quality result. Make sure to document what was done, what aspects worked, and how these devices impacted your organization. Don't be afraid to include those activities that failed, since the idea may come up again and your review may save the committee from wasting time moving in the wrong direction. You may be surprised at the amount of work the committee has completed.

If you are tracking measurable results with a scientific analysis as suggested in point 5 above, include this in your annual review. In fact, your internal documentation can provide you with the data you need to submit to national contests for excellent ESOP communication, such as the Annual Awards for Communication Excellence (AACE) through the ESOP Association or the Innovations in Employee Ownership Award through the National Center for Employee Ownership (NCEO) and the Beyster Institute.

7. Deep Fry It

Here's proof that I'm from the Midwest: I know that deep-fried battered curds of cheese can replace a side order of fries at many fast food restaurants in Wisconsin. If you haven't had deep-fried cheese curds, you're truly missing out. It's an example of thinking outside of the box. Success is found by trying new things. We use cheese in different ways, like adding a slice of cheddar to apple pie or mixing cream cheese with mashed potatoes, both yummy concoctions.

The most popular question I receive is how to come up with new ideas. Being creative with a retirement plan is not always easy, but it is possible. I've heard of very creative ideas over the years, from an ESOP breakfast (serving Eggs, Sausage, Orange juice, and Pancakes) to posting ESOP facts on the back of bathroom stalls as CAN (Captive Audience News). The important thing to apply to your creative ideas is some kind of connection to the ESOP. Some companies use team building activities like tug-of-war or scavenger hunt. If you have a miniature golf game, ask employees questions about the ESOP for them to take one step closer to the hole before putting. Another company features an employee-owner each month so that everyone can get to know their fellow employees. New ideas are always welcome, but remember, if a particular event or activity becomes so popular that it becomes tradition, keep it!

8. Good Cheese Isn't Made Overnight

Most hard cheeses require several days or months to age. Cheeses aged longer are some of the most valuable. In 2009, a 15-year aged cheddar was released by Hook's Cheese Company of Mineral Point, Wisconsin.[3] It sold for $50 per pound. Aging cheese is a process just like the development of your committee. A successful committee requires patience to become comfortable with its roles and responsibilities. It takes time to become knowledgeable about the ESOP. That doesn't mean newer committees can't do great things. It simply means becoming more effective and more valuable takes patience. Don't set yourself up for failure by expecting too much too soon.

In fact, the first activity or event your new committee tries to accomplish should be fairly simple so its members can celebrate its success and build confidence. For example, developing a simpler ESOP statement format might be a better initial task than implementing an Employee-Owner of the Year program. One of the most successful ESOP committees I know, the one at Van Meter, invested at least two years into developing the committee before implementing many employee activities (see the case study of Van Meter's committee in the final chapter of this book). Their investment shows in the great things they do today. In the spirit of spreading the wealth, the Van Meter committee has gone beyond just ESOP communication by implementing community charitable programs and employee wellness initiatives. Great success sometimes requires great patience. Hook's Cheese Company experienced so much success with its 15-year aged cheddar that it is now investing in a 20-year aged cheddar.

9. Cheese as the Main Course

Cheese is typically considered a snack, appetizer, or an ingredient to add to other dishes. It's usually not the main course. However, in early 2010, a cheese-only restaurant opened in London, boasting over 100 varieties of cheese and cheese dishes, including cheese ice

---

3. "After Aging 15 years, America's Oldest Cheddar Goes on Sale," *Journal Sentinel,* December 4, 2009, http://www.jsonline.com/entertainment/78571202.html.

cream, which has become a favorite. To become a main course in your company's culture, your ESOP and its ESOP communication committee need to be seen and heard. Let the committee take ownership of its structure by developing its own charter and mission statement. Members will be more likely to take responsibility for the success of the committee if they are given the responsibility for building it. Promote the committee members in the same way you promote the ESOP; this will create a strong connection between the two. Whenever you have an ESOP event or activity, the committee should be running the show. As employees recognize the committee members and see what they do, employees will go to them with questions. An added bonus is that employees will be curious about the members' activities and will ask how they can become members of the committee.

If you avoid these common mistakes as best you can, your ESOP committee may become a true connoisseur of ESOP communication. Bon appétit!

Part 3
Case Studies

CHAPTER 8

Inside the BL Companies ESOP Committee

Linshuang Lu

Learning about other companies' experiences can be an effective way to gain valuable ideas and guidance on setting up a new communications committee, or to revive an existing one. This chapter illustrates how different companies have approached their employee committees. The primary case study covers the beginning and development of an effective ESOP communications committee at BL Companies. This chapter also draws examples from two other companies, Forsythe Technology and Gardener's Supply, to provide alternative ideas on how different employee committees operate. Each company needs to determine what will work best based on the company's unique characteristics and ownership objectives.

Initial Creation

BL Companies is an integrated engineering and architecture services firm headquartered in Meriden, Connecticut, with 160 employees and seven offices located in Connecticut, New York, Pennsylvania, and Maryland. Its services include architecture, mechanical, electrical, plumbing, civil engineering, environmental sciences, land surveying, landscape architecture, and planning.

BL Companies formed its ESOP in 2006. In its research, the senior leadership team (SLT or "senior leadership") learned that properly implementing an ESOP entailed both fiduciary and communication responsibilities. The SLT believed that the skills and tasks required to fulfill these responsibilities required different people. The SLT first created the ESOP fiduciary committee to manage the legal and financial aspects of the ESOP and to direct the external trustee.

The SLT decided in the following year to create an employee communications committee to facilitate a group of employees who would speak to other employees, representing themselves, and not be a proxy for management. The SLT discussed several potential staff members who might be suitable to serve as the committee chairperson and approached the final candidate, who accepted the position. To make the committee truly employee-driven and empowered, the SLT gave the chairperson freedom in selecting the initial committee members. The SLT also gave the communications committee a vague and broad directive—the committee knew that its purpose was to communicate about the ESOP and then see how things evolved from there.

The communications committee fit into a broader effort to improve employee engagement and encourage employee-owners to take on greater responsibility for the direction of the company. The committee initially focused on promoting awareness of the ESOP and increasing morale, but it has shifted its efforts as the company, the committee itself, and the environment have changed.

Getting Started

Before drafting the mission statement or planning any educational events, the committee had an immediate assignment to complete. The SLT asked the committee to design the ESOP annual statements, make them easily understandable, and eventually roll out a training program to explain them. The committee got started right away on this at its first meeting, drafted some samples, and then finalized an ESOP statement format to bring back to the ESOP third-party administrator (the vendor responsible for actually producing the statements). The committee members also decided who among them had the skills and desire to do the training. (The design of the statement has been continually enhanced since 2007, but many of the original features are still in place.)

Start with the Mission Statement?

Many committees start with a formal retreat to draft the mission statement and goals and to establish the charter, but urgent tasks can take precedence. Starting with a concrete task can energize the committee, as members enter into regular planning with a sense of accomplishment and familiarity with the group's dynamics (e.g., the four stages of committee development outlined in chapter 6).

Getting Started Again

After designing the statement, the communications committee held a two-day planning retreat away from the office and made the decision to have the meeting facilitated by an external consultant. The retreat started with additional training on the ESOP, giving committee members a chance to learn the technical details so that they could feel comfortable educating other employees later on. The committee then reviewed larger business goals of BL Companies to set the context for drafting its mission statement and goals. Both the SLT and committee members felt that it was essential to anchor the work of the committee to larger company objectives so that the committee would contribute to building a better firm.

Drafting their mission statement enabled the members to identify their core purpose as a committee and figure out the focus of their activities. Establishing goals then allowed the committee to specify the types of changes they wanted to see at the company. The committee spent approximately half a day drafting this mission statement and goals:

Mission: To promote an inclusive and interactive workplace by educating our colleagues on our rights and responsibilities as employee-owners, and encouraging pride in the impact each of us has on our product and profession.

Goals:
- Educating current and new employees about the ESOP
- Facilitating two-way communications among all employee-owners

- Encouraging individual and team performance
- Connecting all employees, all offices, all disciplines
- Conveying the importance of each employee's role
- Continuing education on ESOP issues for the committee itself
- Fostering a Shared Ownership Culture—shared responsibilities, workload, resources, accountability, profitability, success
- Promoting the "Growing by Sharing" philosophy

After drafting the mission statement and goals, the committee brainstormed ideas for activities. Because BL Companies had never had an ESOP committee before, members reviewed a number of case studies before the meeting to help seed initial ideas. Then at the meeting, the members created a long list of possible activities without evaluating their feasibility or value.

Following the brainstorming session, the committee used the list they generated to prioritize what they would actually do for the next 12 to 18 months. This process proved difficult, but the members applied a set of filters to the activities to help them establish priorities. The first filter identified what the committee needed to do over the next 12 to 18 months and prioritized those activities. The members then selected what they wanted to do, which ended up as second-priority activities. The committee also asked themselves whether these activities aligned with the mission. This proved to be difficult because almost everything on their activities list could be argued to support the committee's mission, but some activities seemed to be best implemented by other groups in the company (e.g. safety manual improvements or office signage).

This filtering process enabled the committee to draft an initial set of activities, some with greater priorities than others, to develop a rough timeline and to assign each task to a responsible individual. For future reference, the committee also noted the activities it was unable to include.

For the first 18 months, BL Companies prioritized education around the ESOP transaction, annual statements, BL Companies' ownership structure, the design of a BL Companies ESOP logo, and fun and educational activities throughout ESOP Month. Office improvement and beautification, community service enhancement, and "lunch and learn" sessions focused on employee development were placed in the "want-to-do" category.

While senior management did not attend the two-day planning retreat, the committee did review its plan with a few members of the SLT and then presented the draft plan at a follow-up SLT meeting. Members of the SLT offered their observations but did not dictate to the committee what it should do.

How to Launch a Committee

Not all committees have the luxury of a two-day retreat to start their initial activities, but ideally, having a lengthier meeting in person, with several hours of time set aside, builds group cohesiveness. Some companies find it helpful to engage an external consultant in the early stages or at regular intervals of setting up an employee committee, while others find that they can develop their committees on their own.

Drafting an action plan during the committee planning meetings builds momentum for the committee. While drafting mission and goals and deciding on the charter (i.e. a formal document describing the procedures of a committee which may include aspects such as decision-making, member selection, and meeting schedule) are important first steps; having a tangible action plan focuses and energizes the group.

Planning and Regular Meetings

For the first few years, the communications committee held annual two-day retreats. The first day was usually devoted to "looking backward" and assessing the impact of the prior year's activities. Afterward, the committee generally spent time discussing and brainstorming to determine what activities should be continued, what new activities should be added, and what activities no longer needed to be continued or were no longer a high priority. These discussions were enhanced by committee members' own learning through reading and research as well as networking with ESOP committee members from other companies at regional and national conferences.

In recent years, the committee's annual meetings were short-ened to one day (8 a.m. to 5 p.m.) following a similar agenda. The committee also drafts a budget for the activities for the year for approval by senior leadership. The annual retreats allow the com-mittee to assess the prior year's performance, review and revise its goals, and plan for the next year. The committee has made changes to its goals over time and experimented with a short version of its mission statement before deciding that the original, longer version was more powerful.

The committee also meets monthly for two hours to review the progress of its planning. While the committee enters each year with a tangible plan, it often revises the plan based on changes in atmosphere and the success of events. For instance, one year the committee planned four "Margarita Meltdown" sessions that took place in the middle of the day. The event was supposed to give employees an opportunity to speak candidly to one another and to senior management without fear of repercussions. The event, however, was not successful—some people came, but nobody felt comfortable enough to speak openly in this particular format.

How Often Should the Committee Meet?

Most ESOP committees meet on a regular basis, biweekly or monthly, for a few hours to check in on responsibilities and progress. Compa-nies vary in terms of more intensive annual or long-term planning. The employee committee at Gardener's Supply operates effectively with a retreat only once every couple of years to do formal, long-term strategic planning. In contrast, Forsythe Technology runs a two-day retreat twice a year which includes formal welcoming of new members, team-building activities, monitoring, evaluation, and future planning.

Membership Selection and Decision-Making

BL's communications committee wanted to keep an informal at-mosphere and as a result never established a formal charter with guidelines for membership selection and decision-making. The committee uses a loose form of voting for making decisions. In early years, because of differing opinions among members, the committee spent a lot of time discussing what it was trying to accomplish. In recent years, the members have shared more similar perspectives, and decisions have been easier to make.

Because there was no formal process for member selection and member terms, from 2007 to 2011 the committee decreased from 13 members to 8, mostly due to natural turnover—some people stepped down due to growing job responsibilities or simply feeling that their time on the committee was finished.

As of 2011, the committee had selected new members and planned to establish formal guidelines for member selection and terms in the future. For the 2011 selection process, the committee approached divisions or departments that were underrepresented and suggested names of people from those divisions who represented the voice of employees and were well respected by their peers. The committee now tries to articulate expectations relating to time commitment for managers and potential new members—something that the committee can now do fairly accurately after a few years of experience.

Going forward, the committee is thinking of establishing two- to three-year terms for 8 to 12 members, with good representation of all offices and departments. The committee also wants to be thoughtful about maintaining continuity and avoiding reinventing the wheel with the influx of new members. The committee would like to give as many people as possible the opportunity to serve on the committee at some point, hoping that every employee will eventually have a chance to rotate onto the communications committee.

Skeptics have been invited to join the committee. Many act surprised, wondering, "Why are you asking me? I don't like the ESOP. I'm going to be a real pain." These more skeptical committee members end up being valuable to the committee—they represent the questioning voice asking questions such as, "How is this benefitting the senior leaders?," "The repurchase obligation—how is that going to affect company finances?," or "Is the ESOP for real, and what's really in it for me?" More pro-ESOP enthusiastic members may take such questions for granted or overlook them.

Record mtg?

The committee has only two formal leadership positions, chair and vice chair, with the vice chair assuming the position of the chair when he or she steps down. Initially, the committee had a secretary, but it decided to eliminate the position because the person wrote minutes and was not as engaged with the meeting. As a result, the committee does not keep formal minutes, but instead mostly just keeps track of tasks and responsible parties.

Keeping Minutes

Some committees find it extremely valuable to have a dedicated minute-taker. This can often be someone who is not a regular committee member but rather acts as a supporting staff member. Other committees share the duties of note taking, though this does make it difficult to maintain consistency over time.

Relationship with Senior Leadership

Senior leadership at BL Companies has always fully supported the communications committee. As mentioned above, the senior leadership team was very hands-off and gave the communications committee a lot of autonomy. Unlike many other communications committees, there is no senior management liaison on the committee—senior leadership wanted to leave the committee on its own and have it be a genuine employee-to-employee communications group. They were concerned that if someone senior were a member, the committee might be perceived as enacting "the senior leaders' agenda." The SLT also does not give the committee formal guidelines for use of time or money, but rather trusts the members to use their good judgment.

To keep senior leadership informed, the chair of the committee does meet formally every other month with the president and annually submits a budget for approval. On an informal basis, the committee may check in and ask questions more frequently. The budget has always been reasonable and has never been rejected. Senior leadership has been fairly flexible about ESOP activities happening during company time. BL Companies is driven by billable hours, and people usually make up the hours at other times.

Forsythe Technology: Another Approach to Launching a Committee and Selecting Members

BL Companies' communications committee started without much formal structure or senior leadership involvement, allowing the committee to define itself. The leadership selected the initial committee chairperson, then let the chair select the other members and delegated to the committee an immediate task, followed by a wider scope of responsibilities.

Forsythe Technology, an IT solutions firm with 850 employees, took a different approach. The two senior leaders who created the ESOP committee, the executive sponsors, were highly involved. They wanted their committee to come out of their initial retreat with high visibility and an action plan. As a result, the executive sponsors of the committee spent significant time planning and preparing before the committee members were even selected, and they were much more involved in the initial stages.

The executive sponsors drafted the charter before selecting any members. They wanted to be clear about the responsibilities of the committee and what would be expected of its members. Notably, Forsythe created three subcommittees (communications, education, and culture) and drafted specific responsibilities for each of them. Communications oversees ESOP events and integrating ESOP messages into regular company communications, such as new hire orientations. The education subcommittee provides ESOP and business literacy training, and the culture subcommittee gathers employee input on various issues, such as benefits and values.

Forsythe then launched a large internal campaign for the committee, which included emails from the CEO, to get people excited. The company wanted talent for the committee and wanted top performers to apply for the team. Employees nominated themselves and submitted applications with senior leadership, who made the final selection. While senior leadership did keep representation of different offices and departments in mind, they focused mainly on selecting the most qualified and skilled members.

The company later created a legislative subcommittee, responsible for ESOP advocacy at a national level, including meeting and writing to representatives in Congress. This subcommittee formed in order to support ESOP advocacy efforts at a national policy level and to participate in the wider community of employee-owned firms.

The committee also tries its best to plan activities during natural breaks—breakfast, lunch, or late afternoons (i.e., when employees have the most flexibility and client impact will be minimized).

The communications committee members themselves have a much larger time commitment, between attending conferences, planning meetings, and hosting events and creating materials. Committee members try to make up some hours, or do committee work on their own time—for instance, some committee members met in the evening to practice ESOP training—but there is an understanding that they will not be able to make up all the hours. Occasionally, certain members may spend too much time on committee activities, but these concerns have always been resolved.

As time has gone by, the SLT continues to consider how the communications committee should support wider company objectives. For instance, in the past year, the SLT has encouraged the committee to include more performance culture content into their activities. The committee has discussed creating a dashboard of key metrics for employee-owners and will participate in the company's strategic planning process (e.g. the employee survey and feedback analysis). These activities are entirely within the original mandate of the committee but would not have been easy to implement early in the committee's life cycle, before it established momentum and credibility.

Overall, BL Companies has also shifted toward greater information sharing, transparency, and participation. Employees now feel free to stop by and chat with the president, who keeps an open door and a candy dish to encourage conversation. The firm's leadership also holds quarterly meetings to share financial information, strategy and company progress, giving the communications committee more educational opportunities about business and performance improvement.

Events

In the beginning, the BL Companies communications committee needed to provide basic ESOP education to employees, including how to read and understand the ESOP statement. It established a tradition of training in groups of 12 to 14 people to improve dialogue and encourage questions. The groups are multi-disciplinary, giving employees from different divisions a chance to get to know one another better. Because BL Companies is an integrated services firm, effective communication between different divisions is critical for success. The committee often plans activities with improving communication between divisions in mind.

The communications committee continues this education through meetings called "The ESOP Year in Review," where committee members update employees on the health and status of the ESOP. These meetings have recently become more business-related with financial information, especially as senior leadership has been more open about corporate strategy and finances. The Year in Review gives employees another chance to learn about what is happening in BL Companies' business over the past year.

The number and intensity of other educational and celebratory activities vary from year to year depending on other company dynamics. As of 2011, the committee planned one or two events in the spring and one in the summer. Then the majority of its events are clustered in October, ESOP Month, when there may be as many as ten events, ranging from celebrations and social gatherings to photo contests and bingo games. The committee has considered spreading out its events throughout the year rather than clustering them to make them more manageable and encourage higher attendance. Sometimes, the committee has pushed itself too hard to squeeze in too many events. Having learned its lesson, the committee tries to plan fewer events and make each one highly successful, rather than aiming for high volume at the risk of low participation.

The committee also plans many activities for new hires. It first makes sure that new employees hear about the ESOP during their first week at BL. New employees have noted (or perhaps complained) that they hear about nothing but the ESOP during their first week at BL. Then when a new participant becomes eligible for the ESOP, the committee celebrates with balloons and handshakes as well as more extensive education. The committee wants new hires to know that BL Companies is unique and that employee ownership is meaningful in creating a good work environment.

The committee has also become more active in supporting the wider employee ownership community, participating in Webinars and conferences and mentoring local companies with new ESOPs in setting up committees.

Evaluation

Informally, the BL Companies committee regularly evaluates its past activities. As mentioned earlier, to start planning retreats, committee members often review the events of the prior year and incorporate what they have learned from the past into their planning. At regular meetings throughout the year, they reflect on the successes (or failures) of recent events.

The committee also provides surveys after each training session to collect feedback. The feedback has only been moderately helpful. Most feedback has been positive, but the committee would like more constructive criticism. The committee has considered trying to make the questionnaires more anonymous to encourage more criticism. Committee members have also considered creating a general survey on the effectiveness of their work, in which they might ask questions such as, "What messages are you getting from us? What aren't we communicating very well?"

Evaluating a Committee

Forsythe Technology Inc. has taken a more formal approach to evaluation of its committee. The human resources department has conducted two confidential surveys over the history of the committee. The department asked questions about group dynamics, general effectiveness and executive sponsorship and then summarized responses and reported back to the executive sponsors and the committee. In fact, the executive sponsors became more hands-off with the committee after one survey reported that they were too involved.

The company also recently implemented a revised employee survey, administered by an outside vendor, which includes questions specifically relating to employees' understanding of the ESOP. This has given the Employee Ownership Team an opportunity to monitor its progress from year to year.

Going Forward

The committee tries to gauge the firm's atmosphere and strategically plan activities that address and are sensitive to the general mood. It always assesses what activities would be most effective at the given time.

For instance, BL Companies had to reduce its workforce in 2008 and 2009 in response to economic realities. This was a very difficult time for the company, and the communications committee itself lost members during this time. Employee morale was low, with the effect of the layoffs and the lack of bonuses and raises. Employees felt that they were being asked to do more while receiving less in return.

The communications committee shifted its efforts to boost morale by focusing on employee appreciation, emphasizing that the company did value its employees despite all the changes. The committee cut back on fun, celebratory activities, which seemed inappropriate, and focused more on education. The committee also reduced its budget during this time in order to be sensitive to more challenging economic times, and found creative but inexpensive ways to engage employees.

As of 2011, the company has stabilized and is starting to grow again, and the committee has started to plan more fun activities and games. The committee has also reached its five-year anniversary and a turning point in its own development. The earlier years of committee work were easier because the committee could focus on basic education around the ESOP—five years later, most employees already understand it. The committee is now looking forward to determine what more it can do to avoid becoming complacent. Many ESOP committees can feel stagnant after the initial years of ESOP education if they continue to plan the same activities and events over and over again.

The committee's recent ideas have included:

- Sharing more financial information
- Creating a retirement calculator
- Celebrations for people who reach 100% vesting

- Company-wide calendar with birthdays and anniversaries to foster a greater sense of community
- Tracking and sharing other ESOP-related metrics in addition to the stock price, such as BL's contribution to the ESOP and repurchase obligation amounts

The committee also hopes to be more proactive about externally communicating employee ownership with clients and allowing the ESOP to become a marketing tool. So far, these efforts have been informal (e.g. a brief mention in a proposal), but the committee has considered creating an insert about BL Companies, emphasizing employee ownership, to include in all of its proposals.

Attending conferences, talking to people from other ESOP companies, and getting ideas from other employee committees continues to be one of the best ways for the committee to generate ideas. The committee wants to continue to reinforce the link between daily employee behavior and financial results, both long- and short-term. It wants to integrate more of its messages and activities with the company's business objectives. For instance, committee members may want to explore what business targets the company needs to hit before there are bonuses and what employees can do on an individual and team basis to achieve those targets. The SLT likewise hopes to see the committee continue to engage employees deeply in the company's business and to make them advocates for the ESOP. Eventually, the president hopes that the company will evolve to the point that a committee member can sit on the board of directors.

The communications committee at BL Companies started off with immediate action, including statement redesign, training and education, as well as celebratory activities. More informal in its initial stages, the committee has seen the need over time to establish more formal guidelines, especially around membership selection. The committee has also shifted its focus over time as the company dynamics have changed. Both the committee and the SLT will continue to enhance how the committee can best support creating a successful company with a fun and high performing ownership culture.

A 20-Plus Year Employee Committee at Gardener's Supply Company

Gardener's Supply is a gardening supply catalog and Web company with 220 employees. The company has been employee-owned through an ESOP since 1987 and has had an ESOP committee since the late 1980s.

Similarly to the BL Companies committee, the Gardener's Supply committee initially focused on technical education about the ESOP, but it has taken on more responsibilities over the years, especially in gathering employee input and serving as a communication channel between employees and senior leadership:

- Gardener's Supply keeps birdhouses as suggestion boxes in every location. Committee members regularly read and respond to the comments and sometimes even start committee meetings by discussing suggestions.

- The committee coordinates and sends a representative to annual town hall meetings where groups of 15 to 20 employees meet with the company president.

- The committee gauges the pulse of the company through an annual "Brownie for Your Thoughts" event. Committee members go around to each department with brownies. Committee members never go to their own departments so that employees will feel free to speak. Employees then have a chance to speak to committee members about whatever is on their minds relating to work—whether it is department-related challenges, difficulties with reading the ESOP statements, compliments about the business, or questions about the high back-order rate. After collecting this feedback, the committee will either address these concerns itself or pass along the information to another department. Recently, the committee started coordinating responses to this feedback (e.g. the company staff meetings will explain what has been done to address the high back-order rate) so that employees know they have been heard.

- The committee has 10 minutes at every monthly staff meeting to communicate responses to Brownie for Your Thoughts, an ESOP educational topic, an award, or whatever topic is appropriate that month.

- A committee member also serves on the advisory board at the governance level of the company, representing the employees and relaying to the board feedback about employee morale, what the committee is working on, and other concerns or comments.

Because the committee functions as a communication channel, the committee strives for representation of all departments. Many of the committee's activities have not changed over the years but rather have been improved and refined. When the company reached 100% ESOP ownership in 2009, the committee activities took on deeper meaning and investment.

In addition to its activities relating to employee feedback and input, the ESOP committee also plans celebratory activities, such as the annual "Guess the Share Price" contest, awards, and new employee orientations. Notably, the committee drafted and refined an employee rights and responsibilities document that new employees receive, articulating what is expected of employees and what employees can expect of the company—a visible reminder of what shared ownership means at Gardener's Supply.

Special thanks to Wayne Violette, Jared Yellen, and Carolyn Stanworth from BL Companies, Cindy Turcot and Jason Mazur from Gardener's Supply, and Julie Nagle from Forsythe Technology for taking the time to be interviewed for this chapter. Additional thanks to Alix Rabin and Alex Moss from Praxis Consulting Group for taking the time to review and edit this chapter.

CHAPTER 9

Five Case Studies

Tracey Myers, Brian A. Inniger, the Phelps County Bank ESOP Committee, Liz McKeever, and Dave Fitz-Gerald

Van Meter, Inc.

TRACEY MYERS, VAN METER, INC.

Type of business	Distribution
Location	Headquartered in Cedar Rapids, Iowa, with 11 other branches throughout the state
Number of employees	342
ESOP start date	Partially employee-owned since 1993 and 100% employee-owned since January 1, 2005
Type of committee	Communications
% owned by ESOP	100%
ESOP voting rights	Pass-through

Van Meter started down the path of employee ownership in 1993 and became 100% employee-owned on January 1, 2005. This was made possible when the past president, primary stockholder, and current chairman of the board, Jim Hoke, agreed to sell his remaining shares, enabling us to become 100% employee-owned.

Being 100% employee-owned means everyone working for our company is an owner with a stake in our future. As owners, our people are empowered to make decisions, take educated and calculated risks, and do what they feel is right to best serve our customers. Over the past 80 years, we've built a unique culture where every employee is an equal owner in the company, where we value continuous improvement, where we give back to the community, and where every investment we make is made to improve service for our customers.

Today, Van Meter is one of the largest electrical distributors in the United States and has the best people in the industry. The financial strength of Van Meter attests to the company's long-standing tradition and commitment to sound financial management. The future of Van Meter is measured by the hard work and dedication of our employee-owners. Our ESOP provides each employee-owner a financial interest in the company's growth arising from the spirit of teamwork and enthusiasm that have defined Van Meter since the company began.

Mission and Activities

The ESOP committee was formed in 2004. The members of this committee are a group of employee-owners who represent various operating divisions, departments, and regions of Van Meter and are committed to improving the understanding of the ESOP by all employee-owners. The ESOP committee's mission statement is "To maximize the value of our ownership in Van Meter."

The purpose of the ESOP committee is to make ownership at Van Meter meaningful to all employee-owners (i.e., those at every division, every location, and all levels of the company). The committee does this by:

- enhancing the understanding of the ESOP and communicating ownership benefits and responsibilities to all employees;

- keeping employees involved in ESOP issues and encouraging involvement in affecting the performance of the company;

- acting as a conduit to intelligently communicate employee ideas and thoughts to our leadership group;

- fostering an environment of ownership and responsibilities that will be embraced company-wide; and

- organizing and facilitating educational programs and company events that further our mission and the above roles.

ESOP Committee Activities

Guess the Value Contest

The ESOP committee throws an event every spring called "Guess the Value Contest." Everyone in the company has a chance to guess what Van Meter's stock value is. The contest winner receives 10 times the amount of the stock value. There is also a traveling trophy that the winner displays for the entire year.

Work 10 Years and Get 5 Years Free

Recently, the ESOP committee rolled out a "Work 10 Years and Get 5 Years Free" campaign. This was a way to help employee-owners understand more about their future with ESOP and to help them think about longevity with the company. An example was given to the employee-owners using a median employee salary and ESOP account balance and some "what if" numbers assuming there would be a nice annual contribution and stock growth. Those numbers show that an employee who works for 10 years at Van Meter may well have an ESOP account worth the equivalent of 5 years' salary. This campaign has been effective and is continuing to help employee-owners understand the effect they can have on growing the company and their future.

Super-Sized Gain Share

The ESOP committee rolled out a "Super-Sized Gain Share" program in 2006 with a goal of motivating employee-owners to beat gross profit (GP) goals each month. To do this, Van Meter gives monthly monetary rewards based on how many percentage points we are above our GP goal for the month. Beating GP goals is one of the best ways to keep our stock price growing.

"I'm In" Meeting

After new hires reach their six-month anniversary, the company throws an "I'm In" Meeting, celebrating their official initiation into the ESOP. During this meeting, we provide fact sheets on the basics of the plan, educate the new employee-owners on the history and value of our ESOP, and inform them of tools they can use to better understand the ESOP (an example is an ESOP link at our intranet site, where we keep all of our information electronically).

Employee Ownership Month

Each October, Van Meter celebrates Employee Ownership Month with a different theme. In 2010, the theme was ESOPtoberfest. We had brats and root beer at an employee celebration lunch to go along with our theme. We also had many activities to encourage employee-owners to become more involved with employee ownership. Each year we also hold an ESOP poster contest. We use the same guidelines as the AACE awards (the Annual Awards for Communications Excellence, sponsored by the ESOP Association) and enter our winner in the national contest. In 2010, we had more than 90 employee-owners submit poster entries for our contest and it took the committee a full day to narrow it down to three finalists. After the three finalists were chosen, we sent out voting ballots to all employee-owners, who then voted on the winning poster concept. Each year, the winner receives $1,000, the two semi-finalists receive $100, and all of the remaining entries go into a drawing for 10 gift cards worth $50.

Stock Value Presentation

The ESOP committee holds an annual ESOP statement roundtable discussion at all locations, where we announce the contributions and stock price, and educate one another on the company valuation. We also give history education and try to build on financial literacy from year to year. The roundtable discussions typically have anywhere from five to a dozen employees at each sitting so that an environment is created where intimate questions can be asked and plenty of time can be spent with each employee-owner on education.

ESOP Committee Structure

The ESOP committee has 11 members, all of whom are elected to the committee by all employee-owners. Representation is proportionate to the number of employees in each of our business units. There are also non-elected representatives also on the committee including a person from finance, operations, marketing, and learning and development.

Members of the committee are elected via a nomination and/or volunteer process within business units or departments they serve, followed by a vote. The person or persons receiving the highest number of votes are elected to the committee. In the event of a tie, a runoff election is held to determine the winner. In the event of a tie in the runoff, the members of the ESOP committee votes to break the tie.

Each committee member serves a three-year term. The committee members' terms are staggered in an effort to keep continuity within the group. The officers of the committee include a president, president-elect, treasurer, secretary, and historian. Each officer serves a one-year term on the committee. The officers are elected by nominations from the committee followed by a vote. This occurs at the last committee meeting of the year.

Responsibilities of Committee Members

- *President:* Schedules and sets the agenda and presides over the committee meetings.

- *President-elect:* Responsible for filling vacancies on the committee by notifying the department heads of the vacancies and monitoring the election process. Also assists the president in all endeavors and prepares for his/her term of office as president. The president-elect becomes the president if the president resigns or is removed.

- *Treasurer:* Records the committee spending and gives a report at the committee meetings.

- *Secretary:* Records and distributes the minutes from the meetings and has them posted on the Van Meter intranet.

- *Historian:* Responsible for gathering and archiving information from events and meetings. The historian is also responsible for keeping the Van Meter commemorative album up-to-date for use in new employee orientations and other special events.

Communications

At Van Meter, our purpose is to be our customers' competitive advantage. We do this by creating a culture where the right people come to work, stay, and achieve their potential. Our culture is extremely important to us and we try to operate with regard to our core beliefs. These beliefs influence how we communicate throughout the company.

Our Beliefs (5P's: People, Profit, Place, Provide, and Continuous imProvement)

- We have a culture that is committed to the development and well being of our **people**. In 2009 and 2010 we sent out an employee engagement survey to all employees. Van Meter's engagement level in 2010 was 58.6%, which is 27% above the national average for employee engagement.

- We don't run the business to make a profit . . . we make a **profit** to run the business. Each year, a portion of Van Meter's profits are allocated to our three business regions' charitable giving committees. The committees then decide where the money would be best placed throughout different organizations in their communities.

- We are blessed by our communities and our **place** in them. We support our communities with our time, talents, and monetary treasures. In 2010, Van Meter employees volunteered 8,797 hours.

- We strive to take care of those who **provide** us the opportunity to be in business. As employee-owners, we are encouraged to create innovative solutions for our customers and suppliers, which is what keeps us in business. This sense of confidence and trust is what we value in our culture.

- **Continuous imProvement** is essential for our future. We believe in improvements happening every day, from everyone. In 2010, our goal for each employee was to submit two Quick Kaizens, which are ideas that improve the efficiency, safety and/or quality of our business.

The ESOP committee communicates to the employee-owners of Van Meter through a variety of mediums.

LiveWIRE

The LiveWIRE is a bi-weekly, internal, email newsletter that is sent out to employee-owners. It informs employees of news and upcoming events, and provides insights into the lives of fellow employee-owners. One of the topics included in the LiveWIRE is an ESOP section. Committee members submit answers to frequently asked questions, announce any upcoming ESOP events, and provide general facts about Van Meter's ESOP plan.

Celebration Meetings

Once a month, Van Meter holds a celebration meeting at each of our 12 branches. The purpose of this meeting is to communicate company updates, announce the company's financial performance for the previous month, and discuss our sales goals for the next month. These meetings are also a chance for everyone to be in the same room and catch up with those they don't see on a daily basis.

Posters

The ESOP committee hangs up posters at all of the branches when it's time for the poster contest and when it's time for the stock presentations in the spring.

Web Site

In 2010, Van Meter's Web site was completely redesigned. We wanted to make sure that our Web site accurately reflected how important employee ownership and culture is to Van Meter's employees. Our culture is what allows us to be successful as a business because when you have the right people coming to work every day and an environment that fosters employee empowerment and decision making, the rest tends to fall into place. To accomplish this feeling on our Web site, we included videos of employee-owners talking about why they like working at Van Meter and what employee ownership means to them, and we included a page solely on the culture at Van Meter and our employee ownership.

Ongoing Challenges

Every day, members of the ESOP committee strive to keep employee-owners educated about the value of our ESOP. We face the challenge of keeping not just tenured employee-owners but also newly hired employees engaged in the plan, especially the younger generation. These young employee-owners are just starting their career and are at the beginning of a new phase in life. For many of them, retirement is not at the forefront of their minds, making it hard to connect with them about the ESOP. Bridging the generation gap and trying to find ways to keep the ESOP information meaningful and interesting is one of the toughest challenges we face as a company.

Another challenge we face is how to keep the activities we are doing and information we are sharing fresh year after year. The ESOP committee devotes a lot of time to brainstorming new ways to share information about the ESOP and what types of activities will engage all generations.

Rieth-Riley Construction Co., Inc.

BRIAN A. INNIGER, *RIETH-RILEY CONSTRUCTION*

Type of business	Heavy/highway contractor
Location	Corporate headquarters is located in Goshen, Indiana, with other locations throughout Indiana and Michigan
Number of employees	400 non-union and 1,600 union at the peak of the construction season
Type of committee	Administrative
ESOP start date	1986
% owned by ESOP	100%
ESOP voting rights	The company has two different classes of ESOP stock with different voting rights, due to legal rules in force at the time the stock was acquired by the ESOP: Class A stock (pre-1987) has limited pass-through voting rights; Class B stock has full pass-through voting rights

Albert R. Rieth founded Rieth-Riley in 1916 in Goshen, Indiana. After his death in 1954, leadership of the company passed to his three sons, Blair, Lee, and William. Upon the death of one brother, the remaining brothers began to consider ownership succession plans. They wanted to ensure that the business would continue and that something was given back to the employees who had contributed to the growth and development of the company. The future of Rieth-Riley dramatically changed in December 1985 with the formation of the Rieth-Riley ESOP.

Mission and Activities

The Rieth-Riley ESOP committee's mission is to both interpret the plan and oversee administration of the ESOP, consistent with applicable law. The committee makes all determinations as to a participant's right to a benefit provided under the plan; prepares and distributes appropriate information; provides annual reports to the board of directors; and employs outside help, such as legal and other professional services. The board of directors and the officers of the company determined this mission.

Committee Structure

There are four members on the committee. Initially, the ESOP committee was comprised of only officers. After a period of time, a nonofficer employee was added to the committee to promote more employee involvement and to help educate employees about the plan and related issues.

The ESOP participants elect the nonofficer employee member to the committee. The election process begins with each Employee Participation Group (EPG) soliciting nominees from its group. Each permanent Rieth-Riley location has an EPG representative. An EPG can nominate only one candidate for the position. If more than one candidate within an EPG runs for the position, that EPG holds a primary election to reduce the number of candidates to one. Once the EPG candidates are submitted, a company-wide primary is held to reduce the number of candidates to three. Then a final election is held to determine the finalist. The board of directors then appoints three officers and approves the finalist to serve on the ESOP committee.

The board of directors determines the length of the term for each office. Officers are appointed for one-year terms and can serve consecutive terms if appointed. It was determined that the nonofficer member should serve a two-year term to increase his or her ESOP knowledge. This gives the nonofficer member a chance to gain the knowledge necessary to provide meaningful input on the committee. This nonofficer member can serve consecutive terms if re-elected by the ESOP participants and approved by the board.

In order to promote participation by other employees on the committee, the nonofficer member shares the importance of the position with those who are interested. Since committee activities can be somewhat confidential, communication by the nonofficer member to the employees about the importance of the position is critical for increased participation.

There is no formal training for committee members, but time is spent during the year and during committee meetings to educate each of the members. This is done through the company ESOP attorney, ESOP appraiser, trustee, and former committee members. The committee members also attend local and national ESOP conferences and seminars when relevant. The ESOP committee meets quarterly, or as needed, on company time. The committee does not have a budget, as the senior officers serve on the committee and approve expenditures.

Communications

Communication between the ESOP committee and the employees occurs through the nonofficer committee member, who sometimes issues a written update to the employees on issues discussed, unless they are confidential. When requested, the nonofficer member makes a presentation at the quarterly EPG chair meeting. This is a meeting among EPG-elected chairs, officers, and management of the company to discuss company business and any other issues of concern. The ESOP committee also encloses a letter summarizing the valuation results and the company's performance measures that affected the valuation with each employee's ESOP statement.

If an employee has a concern about an ESOP issue, he or she can communicate such concerns directly to any of the committee members or through his or her EPG representative.

Ongoing Challenges

The ESOP committee faces many challenges as the ESOP continues to mature and grow. Some of the main challenges include the ESOP repurchase obligation, continued ESOP participant involvement, and increasing the knowledge base of committee members. The issues involved with an ESOP are not simple. Usually, most issues are intertwined with fiduciary obligations and regulatory guidelines. It takes a lot of time and experience for an employee to understand a fiduciary's role in the ESOP.

Another challenge for Rieth-Riley is that the company is geographically dispersed throughout several states. This presents continuing challenges for communicating and promoting our ESOP to all ESOP participants. The company continues to work on effectively communicating to employees the issues that the ESOP committee addresses. In order to promote participation by other employees on the committee and to give the employees' confidence that their plan is managed properly, communication with the employees is essential. However, this effort becomes more difficult since the issues addressed by the committee at time are confidential.

In addition, it creates challenges for the nonofficer committee member. When the nonofficer committee member is from a location that is not close to company headquarters, people must become more flexible in planning meetings. In these situations, meetings may be conducted via conference call. However, the more technical and complicated an issue is, the more important it becomes to hold the meeting in person. This requires very committed people since they may sometimes have a four- to eight-hour drive for a meeting in addition to their normal job responsibilities.

The committee also continually works to ensure it retains the most qualified trustee, valuator, legal advisor and recordkeeper. One of the committee's major strengths is its relationship with the ESOP advisors. The committee has a solid relationship with the ESOP appraiser. Rieth-Riley's appraiser understands the construction industry and its particular business cycles, which helps in the valuation process.

The EPGs are also one of Rieth-Riley's greatest strengths. These groups provide employees with the opportunity to discuss company business and offer ideas and suggestions for improvement.

Phelps County Bank

THE PHELPS COUNTY BANK ESOP COMMITTEE

Type of business	Commercial bank
Location	Rolla, Missouri
Number of employees	85
Type of committee	Communications
ESOP start date	January 1, 1980
% owned by ESOP	100%
ESOP voting rights	Limited pass-through

After establishing its ESOP, Phelps County Bank (PCB) had difficulty getting the line staff involved and interested in learning about the plan. Nonmanagement employees were reluctant to go to management with questions or to have something explained. Managers felt that employees would be more likely to seek answers from a peer. They met with a core group of employees who had expressed interest in learning about the ESOP and were concerned about the apathy of many of their fellow employees.

The outcome was to create an ESOP committee with both management and nonmanagement employees to improve communications about the ESOP.

Mission Statement

The ESOP committee's mission is to educate the employee-owners about the ESOP and the company, to create an environment of shared ownership, and to encourage camaraderie among the different locations. Our vision is to teach the power of the ESOP and continue to inspire a culture of true employee ownership. This mission and our vision statement were determined through joint meetings between management and the employee group.

Committee Structure

The committee has seven members who serve three-year staggered terms. Since the inception of the ESOP committee in 1988, we have restructured twice. Initially, the committee included three appointed management members and three other members elected by the employees. Over time, management was phased out, and employees elected all of the committee members. In 2010, the ESOP committee was structured to include someone from each branch/department to be elected to the committee. These employees are elected by fellow coworkers through campaigning within their department/branches during employee ownership month in October. The committee elects its own chairperson, vice-chairperson, secretary, and treasurer. In 2011, we added the position of committee photographer.

New committee members attend a six-week class that covers different elements of an ESOP, its tax advantages, how distributions are made, the history of the bank and the ESOP, and so on. These sessions are taught by our own CEO ("Certified Employee Owner") trainers. The training gives committee members a more thorough understanding of the ESOP, allowing them to communicate more easily with the other employee-owners. Committee members, particularly newer members, attend employee ownership conferences to increase their knowledge and to learn about what other companies are doing. The ESOP training they receive familiarizes them with ESOP terminology and concepts beforehand so that they can take full advantage of the meetings.

Being a representative of the ESOP committee takes hard work, time, effort, and commitment. In 2011, each member received a $1,000 stipend for each year served on the committee. Also, to represent our bank at functions and conferences, each committee member receives two ESOP committee shirts and one ESOP committee jacket.

Communications

Communications between committee members and the rest of the employees happen at staff meetings, via email, and through informal conversations. The many imaginative ways in which PCB builds excitement about the ESOP, celebrates its successes, and involves its employee-owners on a day-to-day basis foster continuous two-way communication.

Meeting Events

Involving people in the ESOP is an ongoing challenge, and if PCB has learned anything over the years, it is that everything runs its course. What worked well as far as training and cheerleading last year may not work this year. That is why the ESOP committee's annual retreat is so important, to set our goals for the coming year, and plan the activities to accomplish those goals.

The planning retreat is normally held away from the bank at the beginning of a new ESOP committee term, which starts in November. The meeting involves gathering for a full day to discuss what the events will be for the upcoming year, what type of activities/ games the committee will do, what the theme for the year will be. For example, last year's theme was "The Past, Present and Future," and the 2011 theme is "We Are a Better Team Because of You!" The committee puts together the ESOP plan and budget for the coming year. Senior management believes as employee-owners we have the knowledge and understanding how the expenses affect the bottom line, so in 2011 the ESOP committee budget was eliminated.

The committee usually meets once a month unless it is planning a special event that requires more frequent meetings. Most meetings are held on company time, but some events, such as the planning retreat, are done on personal time.

Each year the ESOP committee attends the meeting with our bank's accounting firm and executive committee to review financials for the bank, Phelps County Bancshares, and the ESOP. At this meeting we will learn the stock price for the current year and begin the stock guessing game bank-wide. The winner receives a day off with pay and is announced at the annual shareholders dinner.

To keep the committee energized and continue the opportunity to establish networks with other ESOP companies, the ESOP members attend various meeting throughout their terms. Afterward, they share the information with their fellow committee members and with the PCB staff at the quarterly meetings.

Welcoming New Employee Events

The ESOP committee is involved with new employee orientation. Before an employee's first day of work, the ESOP committee sends the new employee a welcome letter. Enclosed within the letter is a picture of the ESOP committee and their business cards. Within the first week of employment, two ESOP members take the new employee out to lunch to discuss our ESOP and answer any questions. We call this a "buddy lunch." However, in the beginning, emphasis is placed on learning the new job and understanding the ownership culture. In-depth ESOP education starts about six months later.

Every year the ESOP committee hosts an ESOP new-employee breakfast for any employee hired the prior year. Our CEO gives the presentation of the fundamentals of ESOPs and what it means to be an employee-owner of our bank. This event is attended by the ESOP committee and a representative from the CEO trainers and a member of senior management.

ESOP Activities

Ongoing ESOP committee activities include, among others, planning Employee Ownership Month activities, planning and conducting quarterly ownership meetings, conducting new employee orientation and vesting recognition, and generating ideas to keep employees involved in the ESOP all year long.

Employee Ownership Month provides an opportunity to celebrate at PCB. The ESOP committee members plan something for each Friday in October to build excitement for the ESOP committee election, which takes place during the fourth week in October. For example, they may bring in bagels one morning or provide ice cream at lunchtime. In some years, Employee Ownership Month has culminated in a main event hosted by the ESOP committee. Some of the favorite events were hayrides, casino parties, cook-offs, fishing derbies, and wiener roasts.

One recent activity was an ESOP Mardi Gras parade. Employees had a chance to earn mask supplies throughout the year by correctly responding to trivia and games relating to ESOP via email. The teams created masks that were worn and paraded by a selected team member. Employees voted for the most creative and flamboyant mask, with the winning team receiving a pizza party. Another year the committee held an "ESOP Bucks Auction." Employees had a chance to earn "ESOP bucks" throughout the year. For example, they could earn bucks by responding to trivia contests in the newsletter within a certain timeframe. People then used their accumulated stash of ESOP bucks to bid on items at the auction. The prizes ranged from a chef's knife to a TV to a day off with pay (the most popular item). Over the years we have held events based on popular game shows such as "Who Wants to be a Millionaire," "Jeopardy," "Money Drop," and "Let's Make a Deal."

The ESOP committee hosts the annual shareholder's dinner, which is probably the most important event of the year. It is a time for the employees and their spouses to enjoy an evening of good food and good information, and to receive their annual ESOP statements. At this event a plaque is given to employees who have reached their seventh vested year to recognize them for their hard work and dedication.

Ongoing Challenges

A lack of time prevents some employees from getting more involved. Long banking hours coupled with busy family commitments put time for planning and carrying out projects at a real premium.

Additionally, teaching people about the company financials is a challenge. PCB's employee-owners have daily access to the financials, and the month-end balance sheet is reviewed at department meetings. The president of the bank also contributes to the monthly newsletter, summarizing the financials and explaining any discrepancies regarding performance versus budget. The goal is for employees to be able to track deposits, loans, and delinquency without having to rely on someone else to explain the data.

Financials are explained by focusing on a single dollar of income, examining where the money comes from and where it goes. Breaking the financials down this way makes them easier to grasp. Creative thinking like this is where PCB excels.

The ESOP committee does a great job at explaining what it really means to be an ESOP participant and what it can mean to the participants' future security. The committee also continues to be very successful at communicating the company's annual accomplishments and encouraging interaction between all levels of employees.

The Braas Company

LIZ McKEEVER

Type of business	Distribution
Location	Eden Prairie, Minnesota (main facility), with additional branch locations in Wisconsin, South Dakota, Florida, Illinois, Iowa, and Nebraska
Number of employees	Approximately 90
Type of committee	Communications
ESOP start date	December 1986
% owned by ESOP	Approx. 83%
ESOP voting rights	Pass-through

When the J.E. Braas Company's owner, Jim Braas, was ready to retire, he wanted to sell the company to the people who had contributed to his success. The rest of the management team at the time was also nearing retirement, and the up-and-coming managers were raising families and were unable to raise the funds to buy the company as individuals. Braas decided to sell the company to the employees through an ESOP. Beyond the potential tax benefits of the transaction, Jim Braas had a sincere and passionate desire to reward his employees for their contributions and wanted to offer them an opportunity to further benefit from the company's success.

Mission and Activities

The ESOP committee at Braas is called the Employee Ownership Committee (EOC). Its role is to help Braas employee-owners understand the concepts, risks, and benefits of their KSOP. (The company combines its ESOP and a 401(k) plan.) The EOC also tries to teach employees how they individually can enhance the company's performance.

At the outset, the EOC determined its own mission. EOC members brainstormed issues such as "Why are we here?" "What is our main function?" "Who is our audience?" and "What results do we want to achieve?" The EOC does not become involved in human resource issues such as pay and personnel decisions.

Over time, the committee has focused increasingly on company culture issues. Braas believes it is important for all employee-owners to recognize their responsibility to think and act like owners. Braas wants employees to understand that it is only by working together toward a common goal that the company will grow and prosper. The ultimate goal is to increase the value of the company so each employee can look forward to a nice retirement benefit.

Braas celebrates its employee ownership status throughout the year with social events such as a holiday party and picnics, but also by seeking employee input on certain business matters. The EOC orchestrates the role and responsibilities for the employee appointed representative, an employee-owner who serves as a conduit of communication between other employee-owners and the board of directors. The EOC also works closely with the trustees, two of whom also serve on the committee.

The CEO Program (Formerly Known as the BUDDY Program)

In 1995, Braas created its "Certified Employee Owner" or CEO/ Buddy Program, an extensive training program that the EOC both develops and administers. In order to become a CEO, employees complete a five-part training program that covers the mechanics of the ESOP, financial training, valuation issues, company culture, and general company operations. Braas wants all employees to understand employee ownership and understand the basics of business at Braas. By educating all employees on the business, Braas hopes it will help them in making better business decisions in their particular jobs. The CEO Program covers the following topics:

Mechanics of the ESOP

- Simple definitions
- History of the plan
- The sale transaction

- Eligibility requirements
- Participation requirements
- Allocation process
- How an ESOP account grows
- Vesting rules
- Diversification rules
- Distribution rules

Financial Training (Designed to Be Fun, but Helps Employees Understand How Their Jobs and Actions Can Affect Company Profitability)

- Basic terminology
- Key ratios
- Components of the financial statements
- Cash flow
- How stock transactions affect equity
- Real examples (linked to personal finance concepts)
- ESOP loan transaction

Valuation Issues

- Defining valuation
- Who determines the value
- How per-share value is determined
- How each employee can influence value

Braas Culture

- Employees' beliefs, values, and behaviors

Operations

- Depicts the flow of an order through the company

Employees in the CEO program are also encouraged to participate in both internal and external activities such as local ESOP Association chapter events and other ESOP company exchanges. Upon completion of the CEO program, employees "graduate" at the Braas annual stockholders' meeting. Graduates receive a CEO shirt, certificate, and plaque. There is an annual recertification requirement for people who completed the program previously. To serve on the EOC, employees must be CEO-certified.

Committee Structure

The EOC is comprised of the president, the vice president of operations and business development, and the human resources director. A cross-section of employees from various departments within the company are involved in subcommittees for various events.

Braas Company's EOC offers its CEO program to interested companies for purchase. Funds from the proceeds of these sales are used to offset committee expenses.

Communications

The EOC communicates its activities and decisions to the rest of the company through company meetings, emails, and posters.

Ongoing Challenges

One of the challenges the EOC faces is keeping the CEO program fresh and meaningful to all employees and providing additional training to those who have gone through the initial program. Providing opportunities for interested employees to become involved and feel appreciated is also a priority.

Committee members believe the biggest challenge facing any ESOP organization is figuring out how to engage all employees in a shared vision for the future.

Looking ahead, the EOC will be focusing on ongoing educational opportunities for employees.

This case study was written with input from Janis Negratti-Samuel. For more information about the CEO/Buddy Program, contact Janis Negratti-Samuel at Janis. negratti-samuel@ braasco.com or 952-937-6473.

Carris Reels, Inc.

DAVE FITZ-GERALD, *CARRIS REELS*

Type of business	Manufacturing reels for the wire and cable industry
Location	Corporate headquarters in Proctor, Vermont, with eight manufacturing sites across the U.S. and Mexico, and a joint venture in Canada
Number of employees	In Vermont, approximately 165; company-wide, 435-plus
ESOP start date	1995
Type of committee	Communication and governance
% owned by ESOP	100% since January 2008
ESOP voting rights	One vote per employee-owner

In 1994, Bill Carris wrote a 40-page pamphlet called *The Long-Term Plan* which outlined his vision for a transition to employee ownership, and his hopes and dreams for the future of Carris Reels. Bill's pamphlet introduced the company's mission and vision. The pamphlet outlined some very specific details about how employee ownership would transpire and also spelled out how profits and cash generated by the company would be used. In the years since, the company has followed this path closely; it took the final step in 2008, becoming 100% employee-owned.

Much of *The Long-Term Plan* spells out Bill's guidance for future organizational development based on beliefs, principles, and values presented on three dimensions: spiritual, emotional, and physical. The spiritual organization is "the realm of faith and acceptance." In this section, the document discusses the Golden Rule; trust; love, caring and enthusiasm; compassion and empathy; and charity. This section concludes with the thought that "spirituality needs to be encouraged and promoted" and that "a power greater than the individual might very well exist within an organization."

Bill states, "we try to deny emotion in lieu of logic. . . . We all have a sense of ourselves as emotional beings, but we have a tendency to deny an emotional aspect of an organization. An organization is no more than two or more people working together to accomplish something. When two or more people work together, emotions are involved." In this section, the document discusses trust, fairness, tolerance, personal growth, individuality, and motivation.

The third session discusses ideals for the physical organization. "The physical tier encompasses the legal contract upon which people communicate. . . . It is real; it is hard; it is substantive. This area is the most comfortable to deal with, probably because we understand it the best." In this section, Bill talks about responsibilities for employee-owners: "the only way to make this work is for everyone to do their share *plus some*. It is that *plus some* that makes this organization different from others." This section addresses decision-making; diversity; ideas and experimentation; measurement and information; productivity, effectiveness, quality, and consistency; customer commitment; and pragmatism.

The Carris Reels ESOP committee, known within the company as the Corporate Steering Committee is, was, and hopefully always will be "the keeper of the flame" as defined within *The Long-Term Plan*.

Shortly after founding the ESOP in 1995, several committees were formed and began to meet regularly. In addition to the ESOP committee, a communication committee and an education committee were formed. Corporate management and site management had been meeting together periodically for several years. In 1997 all these groups were combined into a single committee, which was then known as the Corporate Steering Committee (CSC). The CSC is responsible for communications and training, and the CSC provides value to company management in an advisory role. Management decisions frequently follow brainstorming sessions at CSC meetings. In addition, four categories of decisions are within the CSC's direct authority:

1. Changes in benefits, subject to a budget set by management.
2. Carris scholarship program: award amounts, parameters, and criteria.
3. Selection of ESOP trustees.
4. Selection of the board of directors.

Mission and Activities

The mission of the company is "to improve the quality of life for our growing corporate community." This mission statement headlines a longer, one-page mission statement that incorporates many of the principles outlined in *The Long-Term Plan*. The Corporate Steering Committee has a mission statement, or charter, that reads:

> The Corporate Steering Committee ("CSC") of Carris Reels provides guidance on key issues and objectives of the company. Its membership is drawn from four different segments of the company: board of directors, corporate managers, site managers, and elected employee-owner representatives.
>
> The CSC serves to promote the health and vitality of the company. This is achieved by:
>
> - *Upholding The Long-Term Plan* and the company's mission statement by ensuring they are implemented, reviewed, evaluated and supported.
>
> - *Participating* in formal governance through selection of some ESOP trustees and instructing the trustees on the selection of members of the board of directors.
>
> - *Influencing* a broad range of global corporate decisions.
>
> - *Strengthening* employee ownership culture and values by striving to understand fully all items brought before it, by actively listening and respecting all points of view, and by making decisions based on the welfare of the company.
>
> - *Facilitating* communication among sites by encouraging networking and collaboration across the entire company.
>
> - *Educating*, informing, and serving as champions of a participatory decision-making process.
>
> - *Fostering* provocative discussion to meet changing needs and to position the company into the future.
>
> As the conscience of the company, the CSC creates harmony through effective communication and thoughtful decisions based on expertise and augmented by the input and ideas of everyone within the organization.

The CSC charter document also includes a section on rights and responsibilities. Ten of each are identified and listed side-by-side, as follows:

Rights	Responsibilities
I can expect that my opinion will be respected.	I will respect the rights of others to their opinions.
I can expect a safe and friendly workplace.	I will contribute to a safe and friendly workplace.
I will share in the financial and other benefits of the company.	I will contribute to the financial success of the company, primarily by doing my job safely and efficiently.
I can influence decision-making through my own job and through input to the CSC.	I will provide constructive suggestions if I have concerns and provide input to the CSC at the company-wide level.
I can vote on key issues affecting the company as defined in the ESOP.	I will strive to learn about the business and to grow personally and professionally.
I can participate in the formal governance of the company.	I will participate in the formal governance of the company by utilizing and understanding the decision-making process.
I will have access to information about the management and strategic direction of the company.	I will help to achieve continuing improvements in a productive work environment.
I will know about day-to-day decisions being made and who is making those decisions.	I will read decision reports and help find solutions or ideas for improvement.
It is my right to be well informed about the financial health of the company.	It is my duty to be well informed about the financial health of the company.
I can actively support and advance the company's mission statement.	I will actively support and advance the company's mission statement.

Committee Structure

The CSC includes members of the board of directors, corporate management, site managers, and elected employee-owners, a total of 22 people as of June 2011. The board of directors includes two outside directors and three inside directors who are also members of corporate management. The corporate management group includes the president, the vice president of sales and marketing, the vice president of finance and treasurer, the HR director, and an HR manager who is also the chair of the corporate steering committee.

Eight site managers and elected employee-owner representatives ("Reps") serve the company's manufacturing facilities. Generally, every facility has a site Rep. In most geographical locations, a facility is a single building. In Rutland County, some Reps cover more than one building. Facilities with large workforces are represented at a ratio of 1:50 employee-owners. Reps are paid a stipend of $250 per quarter plus $250 per meeting attendance plus travel expenses, for a total of $1,500 per year.

The CSC meets for three days, twice per year, at the company headquarters in Proctor, Vermont. The CSC chair presides over the CSC. The chair facilitates the meetings and coordinates the agenda process. Five weeks before the meeting, the chair solicits agenda items. Four weeks before the meeting, the chair sends out a preliminary agenda. One week before the meeting, the chair distributes a final agenda. Typically the agenda includes corporate functional reports from sales, finance, human resources, and safety, and it also includes site reports by product line, with one site report per site manager. In most cases, there will be at least one very significant issue on the agenda that will take up four to eight hours. Usually the agenda includes a couple of short training sessions. Often there are discussion topics, or proposals requiring a decision, or on topics on which management seeks input.

Through the years, the CSC has evolved. In the early years, the group struggled to build consensus and make decisions. Periodically the group has sought help from professional facilitators and consultants to assist with process, training, or to facilitate a sensitive subject, or subjects requiring a certain level of expertise. Recently the CSC has worked with a consultant to evaluate the CSC and make recommendations for formalizing the purpose and practices of the CSC, and also to reevaluate and make changes to how ESOP plan trustees are selected, trained, and evaluated. Earlier, a consultant provided surveys and training on rights versus responsibilities, and risks versus rewards, and installed a formal structure for making and reporting on decisions made throughout the company. Earlier still, a couple of consultants provided organizational development training, and helped develop a model for how to make a consensus decision as part of a large group. Now the CSC is able to invoke the lessons learned and the models developed, even though a majority of current members were not on the committee when the models were developed.

Reps serve on the committee for three-year terms. Turnover is encouraged, but on average Reps serve two terms. When a seat is vacant, elections are held at the site. Candidates self-nominate. A secret ballot is conducted, and the majority rules. When new Reps are elected, the new Rep accompanies the previous Rep for one meeting whenever possible to provide for transition.

In addition to serving on the CSC, the Reps also serve on their sites' planning committees. Each year the company adopts a strategic plan, which in addition to identifying long-term goals, also commits the company and each site to short-term goals, objectives, and budgets. Each site meets every month with a cross-functional site management team to discuss sales, profits, safety, training, and decision-making. The Reps are expected to be active participants in the planning and review process, and are often assigned specific topics to track at planning meetings.

An early incarnation of the CSC was handpicked by Bill Carris to represent the sites, various shifts, and different levels of authority in the company. This committee met with counsel before the ESOP was formed and was presented with a list of 18 decisions that needed to be made before drafting the ESOP Plan Document. This group made decisions about eligibility, distributions, and allocation methods. For example, the committee decided to initially have a three-tiered allocation formula that was based 50% on pay up to a $30,000 salary cap; 20% based on seniority; and 30% divided equally. Initially this helped to get a large number of shares into longer-term employee accounts. Subsequently, employee-owners voted to simplify the allocation formula to 10% based on seniority and 90% based on pay, and the salary cap has increased with the consumer price index to over $40,000.

Also very early in the employee ownership history at Carris Reels, each site set up a charitable giving committee. The company donates 5% of pretax profits to a charitable foundation, and each site is allocated a charitable giving budget based on total employment at the site. Virtually the only requirements that each site must follow is that each gift must exceed $100, and the organization receiving a donation must be a 501(c)(3) charity. The giving committees have provided an excellent opportunity for employee-owners to be leaders, and many members of giving committees have eventually become Reps or been promoted to supervisory positions.

Communications

The Reps' major responsibility is to communicate frequently and effectively. Before the steering committee meets, Reps hold meetings with employee-owners at each site to go over a preliminary agenda. At this time, employee-owners can propose additional agenda topics for consideration by the steering committee. Items and proposals for consideration must be delivered to the representative in written format in as complete a manner as possible, and must be supported by a majority of employee-owners at the site. Within two weeks after the steering committee meeting, Reps report back to their site. Because the CSC meetings are so intensive, reporting back is a big job, requiring great notes and an ability to extract the key elements of the meeting. Serving on the CSC, therefore, has provided a great opportunity for personal growth for the Reps. They do a lot of public speaking to represent their constituents both at the CSC and at site meetings, and they have opportunities to meet people from all over the country at external conferences and meetings.

As an employee-owned company, Carris Reels works hard to be good at communications. Carris Reels has won several awards for communications through the ESOP Association's Annual Awards for Communications Excellence program (AACE), but the primary value of the AACE program is for the company to continuously reassess its communications and to pick up tips from other ESOP companies. The company has a formal newsletter that is printed three times per year. Financial results are mailed home in a brief quarterly report from management. At year end, a simplified and condensed annual report is prepared and delivered together with ESOP statements and a "how to read your ESOP statement" page. Employee-owners attending ESOP conferences write trip reports, which are highlighted in the ESOP's intranet site along with training information and archived newsletters. TV monitors in the lobbies and cafeterias broadcast general information and "news of the day." Traditional bulletin boards feature, among other things, formal reports of decisions made throughout the organization.

Ten years ago, Carris Reels worked with a consultant to formalize a transparent decision-making process. The process codified more than 30 different categories of decisions, plus 6 steps for decision making, which include:

1. Initiate process;

2. Gather information;

3. Generate alternatives;

4. Make decision;

5. Inform others; and

6. Review decision.

For each of the 6 steps, a responsible person or party is identified as being primarily responsible for the decision at that point in the process. Each step may additionally have parties identified to (1) alert a responsible party, (2) consult with a responsible party, or (3) have the right to be a recipient of information. The decision report is a formal one-page document that is used to communicate decisions and pertinent information to employees. Company-wide decisions are posted at the site, together with decisions made at the site that are of interest only to employees at that site. From time to time, employee-owners ask for a decision report, which serves to remind everyone to use the system.

Ongoing Challenges

After 16 years of employee ownership, some things are taken for granted. Recently task forces have been commissioned to study some long standing practices. In 2008–9, the entire CSC was put under the microscope. Similarly, in 2010–11, the trustee program has been re-evaluated. In both cases some fairly major modifications were made, though overall both are very recognizable extensions of what existed previously. In both cases, a formal annual evaluation will occur for each. Every five years, the entire CSC program will be put back under the microscope.

Another ongoing challenge will be to avoid complacency—to continuously improve, invigorate, and reinvigorate passions, and continue to evolve and grow.

About the Authors

Jim Bado is the founder of Workplace Development, Inc. He has worked with employee-owned businesses since the late 1980s to communicate ownership benefits. His practical experience includes rolling out new ESOPs, ownership education, team and ESOP committee development, leadership coaching, and strategic planning in an ownership environment.

Stephen Clifford has designed and delivered training programs since 1992, including ESOP basics, employee involvement, financial training, supervisor training, and leadership development. Starting at the Ohio Employee Ownership Center in 1992, he has written many articles and is the author of "An Owner's Guide to Business Succession Planning." He is now an instructional designer for blended learning programs at Babson College.

Dave Fitz-Gerald is the vice president, chief financial officer, and treasurer of Carris Reels.

Brian A. Inniger is the vice president of finance/administration at Rieth-Riley Construction.

Camille Kerr is the director of field building at the Democracy at Work Institute (DAWI), where she directs DAWI's Workers to Owners project, a collaboration of leading actors in the worker cooperative field, as well as stakeholders outside the field, to drive more conversions to worker ownership. Previously she worked as the director of research at the National Center for Employee Ownership (NCEO), launching the NCEO's outreach initiative and managing its various research projects. Camille speaks frequently about employee ownership and has produced and contributed to publications on a variety of topics related to alternative ownership structures. She earned a JD from the University of Cincinnati College of Law.

Kellee Kroll is a consultant for the ESOP Education and Communication Team at The Principal Financial Group. She has 15 years of experience in assisting ESOP companies nationwide. She specializes in helping companies design customized communication strategies and develop ESOP advisory committees that educate employees, promote an employee ownership culture, and help connect employees' everyday work to stock value. Kellee is an active member of the ESOP Association and the National Center for Employee Ownership.

Linshuang Lu is a consultant at Praxis Consulting Group, where she assists employee-owned companies and nonprofits with strategic and financial planning, governance, business education, and ownership culture development. She is a member of the Ownership Culture Committee of the ESOP Association. Before joining Praxis, Linshuang worked at Nonprofit Finance Fund and at Mercer Oliver Wyman (now Oliver Wyman). She is a member of the teaching team for Accounting for Asset Development/Economic and Financial Foundations of Social Policy, a graduate-level course in the School of Social Policy & Practice at the University of Pennsylvania. Linshuang graduated summa cum laude from the Huntsman Joint Degree Program at the University of Pennsylvania, with a BS in economics from the Wharton School of Business and a BA in international studies and comparative literature. She has also completed graduate coursework in sociology research methods and statistics.

Christopher Mackin is the president of Ownership Associates of Cambridge, Massachusetts. Founded in 1987, Ownership Associates (OA) provides strategy and communications advice to companies broadly owned by employees. OA training products include Building an Ownership Culture: The Rights and Responsibilities of Ownership and Frontiers and Boundaries: Managing Ownership Expectations.

Liz McKeever was a project director at the NCEO from 1992 to 2000, working on ownership culture issues, including employee participation and open-book management.

Alex Moss is a founder and principal of Praxis Consulting Group, Inc., where he advises employee owned, nonprofit, and mission-driven corporate clients in fully engaging employees to drive organizational performance. Alex is a nationally recognized leader on shared governance and leadership issues, business and ownership education, communications, and employee participation systems, and serves or has served in many leadership positions in the employee ownership community.

Tracey Myers was a marketing specialist at Van Meter.

Loren Rodgers is the executive director of the National Center for Employee Ownership (NCEO). Loren joined the NCEO in 2005 after working for 10 years as a consultant to employee-owned companies. He is a frequent speaker and writes extensively on many aspects of employee ownership in professional and academic publications. He works with companies on plan design, operational issues, assessment, governance, communications, and ownership culture. He also consults internationally on employee ownership as public policy. He received his master's degree from the University of Michigan's Institute for Public Policy Studies, where he focused on employee ownership in the U.S. and in Slavic countries.

Corey Rosen is the NCEO's founder and senior staff member. He has written many books and articles on employee ownership, spoken all over the U.S. and internationally, and is quoted regularly on the subject in all the major media. Before founding the NCEO in 1981, he worked on employee ownership legislation in the U.S. Senate and taught government at Ripon College.

Virginia J. Vanderslice, Ph.D., is a founding partner and the president of Praxis Consulting Group, Inc. She has spent more than 25 years assisting employee-owned companies in developing high-performance ownership cultures. Ginny is a faculty member in the graduate program in organizational dynamics and the academic director of a leadership development program for CEOs of ESOP companies, both at the University of Pennsylvania.

Jack Veale is the president of PTCFO, Inc. (Professionalizing the Corporate and Family Organization), which advises ESOP companies as well as family-owned or other closely held businesses on strategy, succession, governance, and leadership development. PTCFO provides assistance with management training, management and board retreats, board developments, and organizational readiness assessments for growth or mergers and acquisitions. Jack holds a BS in business administration from Norwich University and an MBA from Boise State University. He is the author of *Creating Strategic Innovation*, a workbook for guiding companies to sustainable growth and profitability using empowered teams.